KNUD RASMUSSEN
THE EAGLE'S GIFT
ALASKA ESKIMO TALES

TRANSLATED BY
ISOBEL HUTCHINSON

ILLUSTRATED BY
ERNST HANSEN

DOUBLEDAY, DORAN & COMPANY, INC.
GARDEN CITY 1932 NEW YORK

PRINTED AT THE *Country Life Press*, GARDEN CITY, N. Y., U. S. A.

Marten unfastened the arrow tips and gave the old mother eagle the sinew string

PREFACE

"THE EAGLE'S GIFT," is a small selection of the Eskimo folk tales which I collected in Alaska during my expedition across Arctic America (1921–1924). It is now my hope that these may bring to one or another—old or young—a fresh breath from a wandering folk who never went out of their way for adventures.

It is an Eskimo from Noatak River who gave the book its Danish name, "Fes-tens Ga-ve," which means "How joy came to man." He was called Apákag and was one of the most lively story-tellers I have ever met. One evening we sat in his house, deep in the heart of a great snowdrift, and told stories. Besides Apákag there was also his father's sister, who was then so old that she never went out, but, after the Alaska custom, passed night and day in a tiny house tent that was set up on the *briks* (sleeping platform). From his old aunt Apákag had acquired all his knowledge, and though she now lay at the threshold of death and only waited for her release, she was far from having lost her joy in the myths of her folk. And this joy we shared. There was one thing we never agreed upon; this was, that I must often break into the thread of the stories to write down what I should other-

PREFACE

wise have forgotten. Apákag sometimes became infuriated and
broke out: "You ruin our stories entirely if you are determined
to stiffen them out on paper. Learn them yourself and let them
spring from your mouth as living words."

He himself had never learned to read and had therefore no
faith in the use of written language. But in spite of all our little
arguments, he it was who finally gave the book its Danish name.
And it came about in this way: One day I asked him to include
all the "Eagle's Gift" tales under one heading, a sub-title that
might give strangers an idea of what was in them.

"You shall call them 'Festivity's Gifts,'" he answered, "even
if many will perhaps not understand that there may also be
festivity in a little fairy tale."

"Why such a ceremonious name?" I interjected.

"Well," he said, "because festivity cannot be enjoyed with
dance and song alone. The most festive thing of all is joy in
beautiful, smooth words and our ability to express them."

In this way the little book received its Danish title, "Fes-tens
Ga-ve."

The tales were, taken down in Eskimo at the story-teller's
dictation, and I have always, in their transcription to a modern
speech, honestly striven to spoil nothing of the fine, poetic tone,
and the artless vigor which is so characteristic of the primitive
spirit and which forms the very pith of the tales. The old hunters,
through the initiative of the Bureau of Education, had now all
become reindeer herdsmen, and the claims of instruction and modern enlightenment were urged with such great vigor that the
traditions from the pagan days of yore were scarcely existent.
My work often demanded of me great patience, but in return I
had also a powerful stimulus: the knowledge that all that should

PREFACE

not now be preserved by careful recording would speedily become lost for all time.

For this English edition I have had the great fortune to obtain as translator the well known Scottish author Miss Isobel Hutchinson, who has herself undertaken several journeys in Greenland for the purposes of study, and who has learned to know Eskimo lands and people at first hand.

To make the heterogeneous material more vital for those who encounter it without previous acquaintance with manners and customs in Arctic regions, the artist Ernst Hansen—who is on intimate terms with Eskimo life—has rendered some of the most characteristic scenes in a series of drawings in which the various subjects are the result of coöperation between the artist and myself.

The Eskimo's surprising power of story-telling will, moreover, speak for itself.

I have always loved fantasy, and have often felt the lack of it. For nothing inflames and inspires like fantasy, fruitful, creative fantasy, which lifts us and leads us up over the heights to the great spaces.

KNUD RASMUSSEN

Hundested,
June 1930

CONTENTS

CONTENTS

CONTENTS

xi

CONTENTS

ILLUSTRATIONS

IN COLOR

IN BLACK AND WHITE

xiii

ILLUSTRATIONS

THE EAGLE'S GIFT
Alaska Eskimo Tales

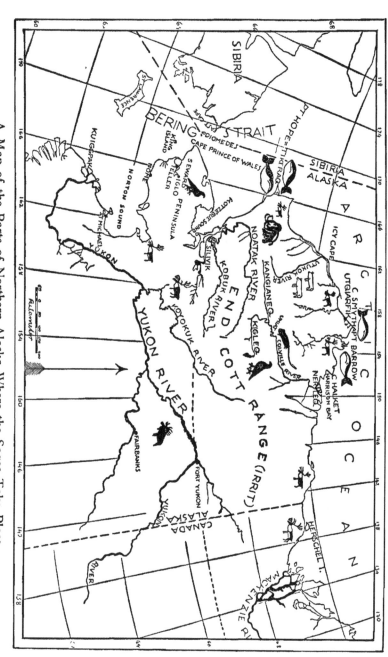

A Map of the Parts of Northern Alaska Where the Sagas Take Place.

KARRTSILUNI

A STORM raging over Bering Strait drove us to seek shelter under the precipitous isle of Little Diomedes, where we dropped anchor just in front of the Eskimo houses that are plastered, more like sea-birds' eyries than like human dwelling places, to the steep cliff walls. The sea folk who inhabit the place are famed for their hardihood, and I had gone ashore to make their acquaintance, when suddenly I noticed a house perched far out upon a sloping brink, yet obviously a more important building than any of its fellows.

I was told that it was a *kagsse*, formerly the feast house of the place, but now inhabited by the oldest women of the tribe. The people had already heard how fond I was of listening to old tales and legends, and a woman offered to introduce me to the village oracle. I wanted nothing better, and off we set.

2

We crawled through a dark entry, reeking of the past, into a long passage built so unevenly that big rocks jutted out everywhere, obstructing our way, as if they would first attract attention to themselves and their own history. Presently we reached the *katak* or entrance to the living room, which is merely a hole in the middle of the floor, just large enough for a man to squeeze himself through by setting his feet on the stone step at the end of the passage. It gave access to a remarkable apartment, big enough to be styled a hall. Walls and roof were lined with rough-hewn driftwood —a trophy of the sea—strange trunks that in their polished lines still bore the rhythmic music of the tides. The planks which formed the floor were so thick that it was easy to see they were intended to bear the weight of many merrymakers. A *briks* (or sleeping platform) ran along all four walls of the room and was so narrow that it looked more like a shelf than a couch. On the walls hung long dancing-gloves, ornamented with red, white, and yellow chips of walrus ivory and the reddish-yellow uptilted beaks of puffins. From every corner grotesque masks, stuck up amid tambourines covered with stretched bladder skins, grimaced at us. In their every crack the timbers held dance rings and feather ornaments— toys only used for those great festivals which are fast becoming extinct. But the pillars of the house seemed to give a sturdy support to all these barbaric adornments which, since the coming of a school teacher with a zeal for reform, have lost their hold over the minds of the islanders.

Not till our eyes had grown accustomed to the twilight did we see, right in the innermost corner, a figure lying

The Feast House

rolled up in some skins. It was Majuak (the Ladder), who was spending her remaining days in the warmth of three blubber lamps at each of which a young woman sat busily sewing

This was in accordance with the spirit of the times, for the feast house was no longer a club for men, but a sewing room for lonely women.

With gentle reverence my guide wakened old Majuak and whispered to her:

"There is a man here, neither a missionary nor a trader, but a man who asks you to tell him a little about the people who lived in our land before the white men came with their new fashions."

In a moment old Majuak was wide awake. But she shook her head and said:

"How can I talk with a man who does not speak our tongue?"

"He says he is one of ourselves," answered my guide.

At this Majuak raised her head and looked at me curiously.

"Where do you come from?"

"From a country that lies more than three winters' and three summers' journey from your country."

At this Majuak sat right up and scanned me with a piercing look.

"You have a white man's face, but you have our tongue. Tell me now, why did folk of our tribe travel such a long distance to find themselves new dwelling places?"

"Nobody can answer that. It happened many generations back, when everything was different from now, in the days when men were still fighting against unfriendly Indians. Perhaps they separated because they wanted to hunt in peace."

"I can quite believe that. In my young days we were still afraid of the Indians and fought them. Many of us left the forests and went to live by the shore. For they say the Indians are always afraid of places where they can't lie in ambush. And so they stayed in the woods and feared the open sea. But tell me now, how long are you going to be with us? It takes time—what I've got to say. My voice is weak and my tongue feeble. I know a great deal—but I must tell it slowly."

"I don't quite know how long," I answered. For I dared not tell her that we had to continue our journey as soon as the weather improved. I saw already that Majuak was one of those true scholars who will go straight to the root of the matter when it is a question of discussing history properly.

Now she answered:

"The man who does not know when he is going to start is surely in no hurry. Very well. But first I must think, for we old folks have a custom that we call *karrtsiluni*."

"What is *karrtsiluni?*"

"I'll tell you that now. But you won't get anything more from me to-day."

Thereupon, with much gesture and waving of her crooked arms, Majuak related:

"In the old days—every autumn—we used to hold great

festivals for the soul of the whale, and these festivals were
always opened with new songs which the men made up. The
spirits had to be summoned with fresh words—worn-out
songs must never be used when men and women danced
and sang in homage to this great prize of the huntsman—
the whale. And while the men were thinking out the words
for these hymns, it was the custom to put out all the lights.
The feast house had to be dark and quiet—nothing must
disturb or distract the men. In utter silence all these men
sat there in the gloom and thought, old and young—ay—
down to the very smallest urchin, provided he was old
enough to speak. It was that silence we called *karrtsiluni.*
It means waiting for something to break forth. For our forefathers believed that songs are born in such a silence. While
everyone is trying hard to think fair thoughts, songs are born
in the minds of men, rising like bubbles from the depths—
bubbles seeking breath in which to burst.

"So come all holy songs."

That was all that Majuak ever told me. In the night
the wind fell, and we continued our journey.

But during our short encounter she gave me, in a single
word, her simple estimate of that humble earnestness that
must be ours if we would indeed let others share in what
arises within the most sacred depths of the human mind.

Karrtsiluni.

Let this then be the message from an old Eskimo woman

—quaint and uncouth—to all who would impart knowledge to their fellows in books, in pictures, in stone, or in any other medium whatsoever. Better motto for his labors no artist can find.

THE BLESSED GIFT OF JOY IS BESTOWED UPON MAN

Ermine Is Carried Off by the Young Eagle

ONCE there was a time when men know no joy. Their whole life was work, food, digestion, and sleep. One day went by like another. They toiled, they slept, they awoke again to toil. Monotony rusted their minds.

In these days there was a man and his wife who lived alone in their dwelling not far from the sea. They had three sons, all spirited lads, anxious to be as good huntsmen as their father, and even before they were full grown they entered into all kinds of activities to make them strong and enduring. And their father and mother felt proud and secure in the thought that the boys would provide for their old age and find them food when they could no longer help themselves.

But it happened that the eldest son, and after a while the

second one, went a-hunting and never came back. They left no trace behind; all search was in vain. And the father and mother grieved deeply over their loss and watched now with great anxiety over the youngest boy, who was at this time big enough to accompany his father when he went hunting. The son, who was called Ermine (Teriak) liked best to stalk caribou, whereas his father preferred to hunt sea creatures. And, as hunters cannot spend all their lives in anxiety, it soon came about that the son was allowed to go where he pleased inland while the father rowed to sea in his kayak.

One day, stalking caribou as usual, Ermine suddenly caught sight of a mighty eagle, a big young eagle that circled over him. Ermine pulled out his arrows, but did not shoot as the eagle flew down and settled on the ground a short distance from him. Here it took off its hood and became a young man who said to the boy:

"It was I who killed your two brothers. I will kill you too unless you promise to hold a festival of song when you get home. Will you or won't you?"

"Gladly, but I don't understand what you say. What is song? What is a festival?"

"Will you or won't you?"

"Gladly, but I don't know what it is."

"If you follow me my mother will teach you what you don't understand. Your two brothers scorned the gifts of song and merrymaking; they would not learn, so I killed them. Now you may come with me, and as soon as you have learned to put words together into a song and to sing it—as soon as you have learned to dance for joy, you shall be free to go home to your dwelling."

"I'll come with you," answered Ermine. And off they set.

The eagle was no longer a bird but a big strong man in a gleaming cloak of eagles' feathers. They walked and they walked, farther and farther inland, through gorges and valleys, onward to a high mountain, which they began to climb.

"High up on that mountain top stands our house," said the young eagle. And they clambered on over the mountain, up and up until they had a wide view over the plains of the caribou hunters.

But as they approached the crest of the mountain, they suddenly heard a throbbing sound, which grew louder and louder the nearer they came to the top. It sounded like the stroke of huge hammers, and so loud was the noise that it set Ermine's ears a-humming.

"Do you hear anything?" asked the eagle.

"Yes, a strange deafening noise, that isn't like anything I've ever heard before."

"It is the beating of my mother's heart," answered the eagle.

So they approached the eagle's house, that was built right on the uttermost peaks.

"Wait here until I come back. I must prepare my mother," said the eagle, and went in.

A moment after, he came back and fetched Ermine. They entered a big room, fashioned like the dwellings of men, and on the bunk, quite alone, sat the eagle's mother, aged, feeble, and sad. Her son now said:

"Here's a man who has promised to hold a song festival when he gets home. But he says men don't understand how to put words together into songs, nor even how to beat drums and dance for joy. Mother, men don't know how to make merry, and now this young man has come up here to learn."

This speech brought fresh life to the feeble old mother eagle, and her tired eyes lit up suddenly while she said:

"First you must build a feast hall where many men may gather."

So the two young men set to work and built the feast hall, which is called a *kagsse* and is larger and finer than ordinary houses. And when it was finished the mother eagle taught them to put words together into songs and to add tones to the words so that they could be sung. She made a drum and taught them to beat upon it in rhythm with the music, and she showed them how they should dance to the songs. When Ermine had learned all this she said:

"Before every festival you must collect much meat, and then call together many men. This you must do after you have built your feast hall and made your songs. For when men assemble for a festival they require sumptuous meals."

"But we know of no men but ourselves," answered Ermine.

"Men are lonely, because they have not yet received the gift of joy," said the mother eagle. "Make all your preparations as I have told you. When all is ready you shall go out and seek for men. You will meet them in couples.

Gather them until they are many in number and invite them to come with you. Then hold your festival of song."

Thus spoke the old mother eagle, and when she had minutely instructed Ermine in what he should do, she finally said to him:

"I may be an eagle, yet I am also an aged woman with the same pleasures as other women. A gift calls for a return, therefore it is only fitting that in farewell you should give me a little sinew string. It will be but a slight return, yet it will give me pleasure."

Ermine was at first miserable, for wherever was he to procure sinew string so far from his home? But suddenly he remembered that his arrow-heads were lashed to the shafts with sinew string. He unwound these and gave the string to the eagle. Thus was his return gift only a trifling matter. Thereupon, the young eagle again drew on his shining cloak and bade his guest bestride his back and put his arms round his neck. Then he threw himself out over the mountainside. A roaring sound was heard around them and Ermine thought his last hour had come. But this lasted only a moment; then the eagle halted and bade him open his eyes. And there they were again at the place where they had met. They had become friends and now they must part, and they bade each other a cordial farewell. Ermine hastened home to his parents and related all his adventures to them, and he concluded his narrative with these words:

"Men are lonely; they live without joy because they don't know how to make merry. Now the eagle has given me the blessed gift of rejoicing, and I have promised to invite all men to share in the gift."

Father and mother listened in surprise to the son's tale and shook their heads incredulously, for he who has never felt his blood glow and his heart throb in exultation cannot imagine such a gift as the eagle's. But the old people dared not gainsay him, for the eagle had already taken two of their sons, and they understood that its word had to be obeyed if they were to keep this last child. So they did all that the eagle had required of them.

A feast hall, matching the eagles', was built, and the larder was filled with the meat of sea creatures and caribou. Father and son combined joyous words, describing their dearest and deepest memories in songs which they set to music; also they made drums, rumbling tambourines of taut caribou hides with round wooden frames; and to the rhythm of the drum beats that accompanied the songs they moved their arms and legs in frolicsome hops and lively antics. Thus they grew warm both in mind and body, and began to regard everything about them in quite a new light. Many an evening it would happen that they joked and laughed, flippant and full of fun, at a time when they would otherwise have snored with sheer boredom the whole evening through.

As soon as all the preparations were made, Ermine went out to invite people to the festival that was to be held. To his great surprise he discovered that he and his parents were no longer alone as before. Merry men find company. Suddenly he met people everywhere, always in couples, strange-looking people, some clad in wolfskins, others in the fur of the wolverine, the lynx, the red fox, the silver fox, the cross fox—in fact, in the skins of all kinds of animals. Ermine invited them to the banquet in his new feast hall and they all followed him joyfully. Then they held their song festival, each one producing his own songs. There were laughter, talk, and sound, and people were care free and happy as they had never been before. The table-delicacies were appreciated, gifts of meat were exchanged, friendships were formed, and there were several who gave each other costly gifts of fur. The night passed, and not till the morning light shone into the feast hall did the guests take their leave. Then, as they thronged out of the corridor, they all fell forward on their hands and sprang away on all fours. They were no longer men but had changed into wolves, wolverines, lynxes, silver foxes, red foxes—in fact, into all the beasts of the forest. They were the guests that the old eagle had sent, so that father and son might not seek in vain. So great was the power of joy that it could even change animals into men. Thus animals, who have always been more light-hearted than men, were man's first guests in a feast hall.

A little time after this it chanced that Ermine went hunting and again met the eagle. Immediately it took off its hood and turned into a man, and together they went up to the eagle's home, for the old mother eagle wanted once more to see the man who had held the first song festival for humanity.

Before they had reached the heights, the mother eagle

came to thank them, and lo! The feeble old eagle had grown young again.

For when men make merry, all old eagles become young.

The foregoing is related by the old folk from Kangianek, the land which lies where the forests begin around the source of Colville River. In this strange and unaccountable way, so they say, came to men the gift of joy.

And the eagle became the sacred bird of song, dance, and all festivity.

Told by Sagluag from Colville River.

AN EAGLE MYTH ABOUT FLYING
SWALLOWS AND A WOLF DANCE
IN A CLAY BANK

BUT men are not content to be like-minded. Some gather and build stories, others forget or misunderstand them. Therefore the legends of different countries are not alike.

In the uplands around Igdlo, which lies on the inner side of that dwelling place called by the white men Teller, one hears of totally different adventures.

A young man, a skillful archer, once shot an eagle which was so huge that it could be divided among the inhabitants as the spoil of the chase as if it were a sea creature. All got enough for a meal, but those who got the thigh bones were the best pleased.

The young hunter, who was called Marten (Kavfiatsiak), realized that it was no common prey he had slain, and therefore he spared no pains to treat the skin so skillfully that the dead eagle looked exactly as if it were still living. There-after he made it his mascot, and every day offered oblations to it, placing meat between its claws each time he himself ate. And the charm worked. He became a still more skillful hunter than he had been before.

One day, when Marten was hunting, he unexpectedly fell in with two very peculiar men. One of them had the snout of a red fox, the other the snout of a white fox, carefully sewed to the front of their fur hoods. The two strangers appeared suddenly before him, stopped Marten, and said: "We have come to fetch you, and since we are not here of our own free will, you have no choice in the matter. You must follow us!" So they took Marten between them and led him into the country, far, far away to regions where he had never been before.

The two strangers were not very talkative, but whenever they opened their mouths they said:

"Tell us what you are fond of. Tell us what you desire. For to-day you will meet one whom you have never seen before, and she will want plaited sinew string from you in return for what she will give you." But Marten did not understand all this. He had no notion what the two strangers wanted with him: he thought they had planned some evil, and he said:

"This is my only wish: let me go back to my home. Give me a good homeward journey."

On they went, a long, long way into the country. But suddenly the two strangers began to hurry, saying:

"We can't get on at this rate. If we are to reach our destination we must set the pace quite differently. Shut your eyes!" And they seized him by the hands and began to run with him at such a violent speed that Marten thought a storm was blowing against them. They never seemed to touch the ground at all.

This went on for some time, and then they told him to open his eyes. They felt the ground again under their feet. Marten looked about him and saw mountains he had never before been near, a strange country, but no houses.

Once more one of the two mysterious strangers spoke and said: "To-day you will meet one whom you have never seen before, and you must know that she will require plaited sinew string from you in exchange for what she will give you."

Marten could think of nothing but plaited sinew string, yet he could not imagine how to obtain any so far from his home.

They advanced further, still deeper into the country, when all at once they heard a strange throbbing, a throbbing which came steadily and loudly from somewhere far off.

"What's that we hear?" asked Marten.

"It is the beating of a mother's heart," answered the others.

"The beating of a mother's heart!" thought Marten, but could not understand what that meant.

Then one of the two strangers spoke again and said:

"Do you remember that you slew an eagle, a young and powerful he-eagle? What you hear now is the beating of its mother's heart."

Marten was still more confused, and an unaccountable fear laid hold of him. What could the two strangers want with him? He had never seen them, and yet they knew all about him. Was the eagle he slew now going to revenge itself?

At last he caught sight of a little settlement with a few houses; here the young eagle's parents lived with a few others. They received him kindly and entertained him outside their feast hall in the open air. Quite a new fashion! But the food was choice, delicate caribou meat, both fresh and dried, with suet. After this he was introduced to the beating heart, the slain eagle's mother. Marten's heart, too, was beating now, but to his great surprise the mother received him with much cordiality and thanked him for the way in which he had treated her son. For it is no sin to kill an animal provided one offers oblations to its soul. Animals live again in a new body. And now she wished to exchange gifts with him and asked him what he would like.

"The only thing I would like is to get safely home. A good homeward journey!" said Marten.

"I desire plaited sinew string," said the old eagle.

Quite at a loss, Marten looked to the ground. He did not know where he was to find plaited sinew string when suddenly he bethought himself of his arrow tips, which were all lashed fast with plaited sinew string. He unfastened them and gave her the string, and the old mother eagle was gladdened and began to talk.

The two young men, she said, were her *kivfai*, her sacred messengers. It was she who had sent them forth to invite

Here the swallows were transformed, and a moment later the
heads of wolves peered out from the holes.

him to this bartering. Marten grew still more astonished, for it was the first time he had heard of this way of sending messages. It was quite a new and unknown fashion.

After this he was merrily regaled with all kinds of delicious food, and when he was at length preparing to turn home, the mother eagle begged him to hold a big dance in honor of her son. The festival should be arranged by his sending out messengers to invite the guests, and those who accepted the invitation should exchange wishes and gifts with himself and his neighbors.

All this Marten promised. And when he at length took his leave, he received two "heart skins" of caribou, tiny little transparent bags, made of the outer membrane that surrounds the caribou heart. One bag was filled with lappets of caribous' ears; the other with lappets of the ears of wolverine and wolf. He crammed the two strange and worthless gifts into his hood, and the mother eagle's last word to him was just as strange as her gifts. "Just take care that you don't lay these gifts down on the way. If you care to take them home yourself, you must not set them down on any chance ground."

This, too, Marten promised, and then was carried off again by the two messengers, the Red Fox and the White Fox, who took him to the spot where they first met.

He was tired after all he had seen and experienced, and when he came to a river flowing between steep clay banks, he sat down to rest.

The steep slope was full of small round holes, and large flocks of swallows skimmed up and down along the river.

He admired their graceful flight and rejoiced in the sight of the pointed wings and cloven tails. Suddenly they all flitted into the holes in the bank. Here they were transformed, and a moment later the heads of wolves peered out from the holes.

Marten sat wondering at all this magic, when the sight vanished just as unexpectedly as it came. He was sitting again by quite an ordinary riverside, but in his confusion he had left the mother eagle's gifts on the ground, and a new surprise awaited him: The small heart skins with ear lappets had become burdens so heavy that he could not lift them. He had to leave them behind and afterwards send many young men out after them; for they had become huge sacks, one filled with caribou skins, dried meat, and suet, the other with costly skins of wolf and wolverine.

These were the eagle's gifts to Marten, because he had treated her son's soul with consideration and offered good oblations to it.

Marten was a young man who had never thought much about anything except his hunting. But after his visit to the eagle he grew silent and reserved and brooded deeply over all he had seen and heard. The aged mother eagle had shown him new customs and asked him to introduce them at his home at a festival to be held for her dead son. Young men were to be sent out to summon folk in the same way as he himself had been summoned; the bartering of gifts, with merry banquets, was meant to create a bond of friend-

Marten's drum was entirely of wood and without drum-skin, shaped like a steep hill with sharp saw-like teeth, just like the pointed tops where the eagles had their home.

ship between distant settlements; all this must take place amid song and dance, and the stuffed eagle was to hang over the feast hall.

Marten thought and thought. For he had not merely resolved to hold a great feast with many guests, he also wanted his guests to share all his experiences. Three other men cast in their lot with him, and the three men sent four messengers out to a strange dwelling place.

Meanwhile Marten busied himself with the preparations for the feast. Everything, even to the beating of the old mother eagle's heart, was to be imitated—a thing to rack one's brains over indeed! But he persevered patiently and at last succeeded in putting together a drum such as had never been seen before. It was entirely of wood and without drum-skin, shaped like a steep hill with sharp saw-like teeth, just like the pointed tops where the eagles had their home. Four pieces of wood were set together, so as to give a hollow space. In the middle of the drum, which looked like a narrow, oblong four-sided box set edgewise, there was fixed a hammer with haft, the sort of hammer one uses to crush marrow bones. The haft was stuck into the drum through a hole, and the hammer head itself, which was also wooden, was bound round with caribou skin. Above the hammer head there was placed a salmon carved in wood, decorated on top with the long wavy down of the eagle. The short heavy drumstick was also adorned with a tuft of eagles' feathers. All this had to be fashioned with great art, so that if one but struck the hammer head with the drum-stick, the vibration of the haft produced a humming noise inside the hollow space in the drum, and there was heard a deep resounding clang, calling to mind the beating heart of the old eagle.

But the swallows and wolves must also be represented. That called for more pondering and even harder brain racking. Marten got over the difficulty of the sloping banks easily enough: he made these of broad boards joined together, in which holes were bored, just like the swallows' holes in the clay slopes. The swallows he represented by dressing the dancers in feather cloaks shaped like swallows with long cleft tails. During the singing they were to dance back and forth till the moment came when they flitted away and turned into wolves. And this Marten arranged by hiding masks of wolves behind the artificial banks, which the dancers could quickly put on when they came in as swallows. The transformation was to take place so quickly that they came out again almost instantly and continued the dance as wolves. This has since become a famous masquerade which is still danced under the name of the wolf dance.

Thus Marten prepared his festival, and he was the first man, in portraying his own experiences, to make men pretend to be other than they really were.

All preparations were now complete, songs and dances rehearsed, and the game gibbets full of meat, skin, and fur. They waited only for the guests.

One day, to pass the time, Marten went caribou stalking. He saw an animal, and crawled near to it, and when he was within range took sight and shot, but the wind lifted his arrow and made it fly over the mark without hitting.

And there was heard a deep resounding clang, calling to mind the beating heart of the old eagle.

Marten did not understand how this could happen to a crack marksman like himself, and he jumped up and ran for all he was worth to find out where his arrow had fallen. Then he discovered that he had shot his own sacred messenger, the man he had sent out on behalf of the eagle's soul to summon the people of a distant settlement to the festival. They had hunted the same animal, and so skillfully had they known how to take cover in this tundra country that they had not noticed each other.

Marten stood there at his wit's end, gazing at the dead man. A great misfortune had befallen him. Deep despair darkened all before him. No one must know what had happened, for he could not cancel the festival. Suddenly an idea occurred to him. He cut up the body, took out its entrails, and arranged it properly in such a way that he could dry it in the wind. When it was thoroughly dry and there was no fear of its rotting, he hid it and went home; here he acted as if nothing had happened. Some time after, the messengers returned to the meeting place, but there were only three, and they told how the man that Marten had sent out had vanished without trace, on a hunting expedition. Nobody understood the reason.

Some days passed; then all the guests arrived and were received exactly as the mother eagle had required. First they were entertained outside the big new feast hall, each one announcing his wishes which must be fulfilled, and afterwards they went into the feast hall to begin the actual festival with banquets, with song, and with dance. But when they were all assembled Marten rose unexpectedly from his place, and went out. A moment later he came back carrying the dried body of his messenger, and set the dead man in the place which he should have occupied had he really been a sharer in the feast. Great consternation spread over all the guests. Silent horror was depicted on every face, but Marten gave no explanation, and the feast began. The inhabitants of the place sang their songs. The dancing and eating went on, all took place according to plan, for Marten was a powerful man and no one dared gainsay him immediately. But the joy in the feast had vanished, there was no merriment. Marten tried to show all possible reverence to the corpse by giving it meat and treating it exactly as if it were living. But haste was already playing havoc with the songs and confusion with the dances, and the first wolf dance ended in sudden uproar and the flight of the guests. For now the sacred messengers had decided to avenge their slain comrade. They flung themselves upon Marten, whom they now knew to be the murderer, but Marten was a crack marksman and never missed his aim. Stretching his bowstring with his left hand, he shot down all his assailants before they had time to harm him.

This was the end of the festival, the great feast for the eagle, where men for the first time represented something other than themselves. And this was the occasion of the first war that ever took place among men.

Thus merrymaking and war succeeded each other. It could not be otherwise. Merrymaking and gayety warm the

mind; it is but a step from wild exuberance to rash be-
havior. But it is probably better so for humanity. For who
would exchange the joy of festivity for the intolerable
monotony which made life so empty before the eagle's gift?

Told by Arnasungak from King Island.

HE IS POOR WHO MUST LIVE ALONE

"HE IS poor who must live alone," say the Eskimos.

Their stories always deal with places where father, mother, and children are the sole inhabitants. These do not know the joy of meeting other men, or hearing of other people's experiences. Nothing comes to them from without; all they can procure for themselves must come from their own immediate neighborhood. And even if they succeed in keeping body and soul together, their lot is a melancholy and desolate one. The young men grow restless and try to escape on long journeys, but instead succumb in hopeless contest with giants and huge mythical animals. They vanish without trace on their long wanderings. The young girls who must remain at home are no better off. They pine for a husband to make them happy. Small scattered houses are lost in a vast country. This is the picture represented in legends, and thus it was when the far-faring birds of the high peaks taught men to seek each other's company and to meet together for pastime. The feast hall—*kagsse*—which in forest regions might be of imposing size, became man's natural meeting place. But festivals could not be held very often, or men would grow weary of revelry. The chase must never be neglected for merrymaking. It was the untiring perseverance of hunter and trapper that justified such gatherings, and no one who failed to procure an abundance of meat and skins could hope to play much of a part when the drum called to the feast.

Men had enough to do. For months at a time they must roam the country after caribou, or go hunting in the mountains after wolf or wolverine from small, hastily erected camps far from their homes. If they lived inland they had to journey to the inhabitants of the coast, to lay in blubber for the winter. Thus absence from their dwelling places became customary. But between the periods of hunting it might happen that for long seasons at a stretch they must remain in their dwellings with no other occupation than that of making their hunting gear, fashioning weapons, and busying themselves with what other indoor work there might be. All this took place in the feast house, where the women never remained beyond the time required to bring the men their food. There were many meals in the course of the day; every man considered it an honor to regale his neighbors, and where there were many houses, people took turns in entertaining each other. For no woman brought meat that was intended for her own husband alone: it must be for all that were with him. Sometimes old men without relatives were maintained in the feast house, where they lived on an allowance and were fed and provided with everything needful by all the inhabitants. One can easily understand what a revolution took place when this indispensable meeting place was first introduced. Such a *kagsse* was not erected by one man like an ordinary house, but by the whole community, for it was not to be the resort of a single man, but of all men; nor was it designed merely for festivity, but for work, as well. In return the women were allowed to keep tne winter house or tent entirely for themselves and to rule there unrestricted and undisturbed. Such a marked distinction was there between the home and the *kagsse,* to which women were not admitted, that the first white men who came to the country very significantly called the latter the "club."

In the two foregoing tales it is related how song and dance came to men's dwelling places at the same time as the feast house. There might also be a particular reason for mentioning yet a third gift of festivity, which came into existence at this time, and which from an inconspicuous beginning has grown to such a luster in the dark firmament of the polar winter that it outshines any other mere pastime. And that is the relating of ancient myths and legends. For it is in the *kagsse* that the ability to give expression to experiences and recollections becomes a great and individual art which revives tradition.

Before the first *kagsse* was built, all story-telling was more or less confined to implanting in the children's minds certain religious rituals. This was often left to the eldest women of the house, who were decrepit in every way except in the use of their tongues, and the myths were therefore reduced, in many cases, to terrifying stories such as we know from our own nursery days; for here, also, it was the grandmother's task to keep a crowd of unruly children in awe by telling them something that might frighten them.

But in the feast house, where the listeners were men and often friends who had come to the place from a far distance, more was required, and the old myths and legends took a new form, founded on and intermixed with personal experiences. So was developed through generations the art of story-telling which I found in Alaska, and it was fully on a level with the best I knew from southwestern Greenland and Angmagsalik in eastern Greenland. Therefore story-telling belongs among the joys which under the name of festal gifts came like a gust of fresh mountain air to the human beings who toiled, bent and blinded in their earthbound instinct for self-preservation.

The eagle myth suggested the great assemblies which in former days united dwelling with dwelling. The festivals began with an ordinary exchange of products, though no one was over-particular about the bartering. But gradually the meetings took on a certain form and, as far as episodes and scenes went, became organized, taking on a character of motley and entertaining play-acting. Thus were brought about the national festivals, the whole occasion of which was the need of trading.

Men regarded it as an honor to be invited to compete in the bartering of wares. Very often they had to be content with accepting goods of less value than those they had themselves given away, but nobody paid any attention to that. It was always regarded as an honor to be able to be lavish and reckless, for it was only the most skillful hunters and sportsmen who could afford this; and it might be considered probable that if a man made a bad exchange one year on another occasion the advantages might be on his side. Every district had its own method of celebrating these feasts of barter; the following description—which is the most common—is taken from the word of

Arnasungag, from Igdlo, Seward Peninsula.

THE BIG BARTER-FEAST

MUCH is changed since I was a child. In those days ships
were few and far between, and we lived as our forefathers
had done. Our food and clothing consisted only of what we
could procure for ourselves, and almost all the hunting im-
plements were old-fashioned and homemade. Now we live
among white men, and when the cold is not too severe, we
wear white men's clothing; every day we eat foreign food-
stuffs, and our customs are no longer the same as before.
Our children are facing new times.

Nowadays, anyone who needs one thing or another goes
to a shop and gets what he wants. It is a man's private busi-
ness and concerns no one else; each person's wishes are
gratified without much ado. It was not so in my young days.
All trade was then a joint affair between different settlements, and as men had no money all trade was done by

barter. But two objects have seldom the same value. So, to satisfy all parties in a bartering of wares, men had to arrange matters in another way. The trading alone was not all, but only a part of the things that could tempt and gladden the people who had to undertake long journeys to show others what they had and to explain freely what they themselves needed.

Therefore trading festivals were instituted, and in connection with them, many ceremonies were considered sacred and inviolable. But the banquet was the main thing; for our forefathers knew that men's minds open when they are happy, and all pettiness is dispelled when men meet each other amid good cheer.

When I was a young man we lived up country a little north of Igdlo. Hunting had been good; we had many skins of wolf and wolverine and red fox. Caribou stalking had also been good, and therefore it was decided to send a message to the "Mountain folk" (Kingingmiut) down at Cape Prince of Wales. By chance we had heard that the coast people there had had a good whaling season and that they had a superabundance of the blubber we stood in need of; they had also walrus tusk and ropes of bearded seals which we could not procure inland. They even had fine white-spotted skins of domestic deer, which they bought from the Chukchis. We were two young men who were sent out as messengers. Each of us received a staff to carry, decorated with eagles' down and painted with red rings of ocher. Each ring stood for a name we had to remember, and the names had to be given accurately, in the order in which we had

All the men, women, and children placed themselves in line and
struck up a song.

received them. At that time there was no promiscuous trading, but the bartering was almost always conducted by two men who for many years decided all matters as they thought best. They called themselves cousins, were opponents in song contests, vied with each other in all sports, and regarded each other as so near akin that during the time the festival lasted they usually exchanged wives.

Early in the autumn we set out and took the trail down over the mountains that led to the sea. Many nights running we made our solitary camp, often in fine weather and comfort, sometimes during storms, when we had difficulty in finding even the simplest shelter because of the blizzards. But we were young and reckless and used to traveling. When at last we reached our destination we were received with great cordiality and treated as holy men who ran the errands of the mythical eagle. We were solemnly entertained, and many meat offerings were made to the originator of the feast. But we were in haste; we had to return quickly to give notice that all had received the invitation and would come with what they could bring on their sledges. The people in our settlement awaited us with excitement and received us as if we were strangers that had come visiting. All our comrades assembled in the feast hall, and with many amusing jests we told them of our trip. It was in the days when there had to be fun in everything men did. Messengers had leave to give all sorts of false information, until eventually, after much beating around the bush, the truth was laid bare. It was a custom that the sacred messengers should hide about their clothing small bits of wood, which gave the number of the sledges that were to be expected. But these bits of wood must never be given up willingly; folk must throw themselves on us and find them in a sort of sham fight. There was always much made of this joke. As soon as the full tally was delivered the window had to be opened—it is always right up in the roof of the feast hall—and through this a tall standard had to be erected with a stuffed eagle on top. To this an oblation had to be made at every meal during the whole festival.

Early in the winter, as soon as conditions were settled and the roads favorable, the guests arrived in a long procession with heavily laden sledges. But for a long time before this, a lookout was kept for them, for they must be received by special envoys a day's journey from the settlement. For this, young men were chosen who were called runners. They had to be the best sportsmen, the swiftest, the deftest, the strongest. They, too, received sacred symbols during the festival, and their foreheads were adorned with strips of skin decorated with eagles' feathers. In their hands they must carry a staff at the tip of which there was fastened a dainty morsel that the messenger gave as a special greeting to the man he was waiting for. As soon as the runners came in sight, the whole procession had to stand still. All the men, women, and children placed themselves in line and struck up a song. When this song ceased, the runners must spring forward with outstretched arms and dance up to the man they were sent to meet. Then they placed themselves behind him, naming his and the inviter's name, and sticking the dainty into his mouth. Thus they conveyed their greetings of wel-

The young men's race to the feast hall.

come, one by one, and as soon as this was done the exciting race began.

All the men who were good runners joined them, and now they were to see who reached the feast hall first. It was a matter of no less concern than the very honor of the settlement; for if the strangers arrived first they had the right to take the feast hall away from its owners. And so the runners set off. Behind them came young women with an empty sledge, to pick up the clothing which the runners cast off as they began to feel too hot. It might happen that the competition became so heated that the most zealous reached the end clad only in *kamiks* and pants, with naked steaming bodies quite covered with rime. On their arrival homage was paid to them with song, with dance, and with feasting.

The larger number of the guests would arrive the day after. Slowly they worked their way forward in their heavy sledges; and now they must all put on fine clothes which had never been worn before. A short distance from the houses they halted and were received by the oldest men and the children of the place. The old and the young went to meet them, to pay homage to them once more on behalf of the messengers. Immediately after their arrival the strangers placed themselves in a long row, the people of the place did the same, and the drums were brought out. The eagle was a creature of the open air, therefore the feast must be ushered in with song in the open air. But as soon as they began to beat the drums, two shabbily dressed, half-naked men would come out of the feast hall with long burning torches in their hands. Their arms were bare, they wore nothing from the

instep to the top of the thigh, and the few rags that hung
on them were skins of old furs with the hair worn off. The
festival opened a new period. Joy makes men young. Therefore these shabbily dressed men were symbols of contrast,
of all the hardships and adversity both camps had contended
with before they could with a clear conscience come together
in merrymaking. Waving their long torches high above their
heads, these strange-looking men would run up and down
along the rows shouting: "This is fire and warmth from our
dwelling. May it thaw you! This is fire and warmth from
our dwelling. May it thaw you!"

Again the drums were beaten, but hardly had the choir
attempted to begin the singing when there came from the
house two more half-naked swarthy men, as shabbily clad as
the torch bearers. With long buoyant hops they leaped in
between the guests and their hosts, mystical, awe-inspiring,
grinning with painted unrecognizable faces. There was something ill-omened about them, for strife, too, came with the
first festival, and therefore they carried bows and arrows,
arrows with sharpened tips. For a while they danced up and
down between the rows, until they suddenly stopped in front
of one of the tallest men, set arrow to bow, and shot it off
so close over his head that it almost grazed him. Instantly
all hands were raised in the air, for with this arrow all that
is evil and dangerous was shot away from the festive season.
Now the merry songs were struck up, and people could go
up to the houses and get the good cheer which everyone
wanted.

The big feast hall was cleared for the reception. One of

Behind the runners came young women with an empty sledge, to
pick up the clothing which the runners cast off.

the sacred messengers, whose head was still decorated with fine feathers, led the strangers in and showed them to the places reserved for them. For, as a rule, the guests had wished for special skins or costly furs, and these had been laid on the floor and became theirs the moment they sat down on them.

At the rear of the feast hall was the hosts' place; but these sat with their backs toward the guests, for they must not look at them before the song had begun. They, too, had wreaths of ornamental feathers round their heads and black stripes over their eyes. That is said to bring luck. Between them sat the drummer who was to beat the big festival drum, the upper rim of which was ornamented with sharp, hard teeth. Behind the hosts sat their wives with the choir; most of the young men had drums, the usual flat tambourines, which would be employed later, during the dance. Almost in the middle of the floor between the two parties, sat a wooden doll, a manikin with pearl lip ornaments, a feather on each side of its head, and a border of shaggy wolfskin around its hat. It was a mechanical doll that moved arms and head and beat the drum when a string was pulled. This was done every time a woman entered.

A mighty stroke on the big wooden drum announced that all were assembled. And now the inviters rose slowly and swayed backwards and forwards with bent knees, straightening up a little and turning slightly round toward their guests at each stroke of the drum, until at last they stood upright with their faces toward the strangers. Now began the song, all hands beating the rhythm until again a mighty, deafening stroke boomed from the festival drum; then all the messengers threw themselves down on their knees and remained in that position with their heads bowed until the tambourines for the dance again set the company in motion.

With this the introductory ceremonies were ended. The inviters stepped forward one by one and sang a song in which they mentioned their wishes; wishes which, however costly they might be, must be gratified by the guests; for when the old she-eagle instituted the festival, she ordained that no one must go away with his desires unfulfilled. The wishes were as sacred as the festival itself.

After that it was the guests' turn to answer, and they now made known their desires. In this way all kinds of commodities were exchanged between the settlements, and everyone obtained what he lacked. This exchange of gifts might last many days, it depended on the number of hosts and guests and how much they possessed. Everything was spectacular and luxurious. Men counted it an honor to excel one another; events took place which they could talk about all the rest of the winter, so it seemed petty to worry if one possibly received less than one gave.

Lastly came the great banquet in honor of the eagle. Everything was provided so lavishly that it could not all be eaten. Five times the inviters brought in all kinds of meat, as much as could be piled up on the floor of the feast hall, nothing but dainty, choice things. All ate as much as they could, and what remained was carried out to the meat gibbets and later piled on the sledges when the meeting broke up.

With this arrow all that is evil and dangerous was shot away
from the festive season,

Then came the guests' turn. They, too, had to fill the feast hall with food five times. Thus fair return was received for all gifts, but with this difference, that the meat of land animals was exchanged for the meat of sea creatures. The gathering might last for weeks. Every evening there were song and dance. The sea folk and the inland folk were to become well acquainted, and relate all their summer and autumn adventures. And the story-tellers, who had here an opportunity to talk to a select crowd of listeners, never neglected the opportunity. But when after a while the hosts began to wish for their daily occupations and the guests found their thoughts wandering back to their own homes, the day of departure was set. Then were collected all the staves, the head ornaments, the decorations, the mechanical doll, and even the stuffed eagle. A great fire was lit, for all the sacred symbols must be burned; they must never survive the festival. And only when they were reduced to ashes might the friends take leave and go each to his own home.

Told by Arnasungag.

A STORY ABOUT THE BEGINNING
OF ALL LIFE

PEOPLE don't like to think. They are reluctant to puzzle about anything that is hard to understand. And that is perhaps why we know so little about the beginnings of Heaven and Earth, of men and of animals.

Maybe so, maybe not.

For it is hard to understand how we ourselves came to be, and where we are to go when we no longer live. All beginning and all ending is wrapped in darkness. How then can we find out about the powers that surround and uphold us, the things we call air, sky, sea; the men who live in houses, and the beasts, birds and fishes that inhabit land and water?

No. Nobody can know for certain very much about the beginning of life.

But the man who keeps his eyes and ears open and remembers what old folks tell him, that man is sure to know something that can fill the emptiness of our minds. So we always like to listen to those whose wisdom is gleaned from past generations. In the ancient myths which are handed down from father to son speak the wise voices of the dead.

Yes, we, who distrust our own slight knowledge, will listen eagerly to these ancient tales.

My own grandmother could tell of some surprising things that happened very long ago. Indeed, all I am going to tell you now I learned from her.

The sky appeared before the earth. It came into existence when the crusts of the earth were already beginning to form. And now I shall tell you of the first living creature about whom we have a story. We call him Tulungersak, or Father Raven, because he was the creator of all life, human or otherwise. He was no common bird, but a sacred and life-giving spirit, the origin of all the world, as we know it now.

Yet he too began his existence in the shape of a man and fumbled about blindly, finding things out by chance, until his destiny and nature were revealed to him. He was squatting in darkness upon the ground, when suddenly he came to consciousness and discovered himself. He knew neither where he was nor how he came there. But he breathed the breath of life. He was alive.

All about him darkness surged. He could see nothing. So he groped about with his hands. His groping fingers touched clay. The ground was clay. All around him was lifeless clay. He passed his fingers over his body and found that he had a face, a nose, eyes and mouth; arms, legs, and a body. He was a human being—a man. Over his forehead he felt a little hard lump. What it was he didn't know. He had no idea that one day he was to grow into a raven and that the little lump would grow out into a beak.

He began to think. Now he understood that he was an independent being, his own master, and quite detached from his surroundings. Slowly and cautiously he crawled over the clay. He wanted to find out where he was. Suddenly his hands came on abysmal nothingness; he dared not proceed.

Breaking off a lump of clay, he cast it into the void and listened for it to reach the bottom. But he heard no sound. Creeping farther from the brink he found something hard which he buried in the clay. He did not know why he did this, and once more he sat down absorbed in thought. Whatever could there be in all this darkness around him?

Suddenly he heard something brushing through the air, and a light little creature settled on his hand. With his other hand he felt it, and found that it had a beak and wings and warm soft feathers all over its body, but small bare feet. It was a little sparrow. All of a sudden the raven realized that it was there before he was, that it had flown over him and hopped around him in the darkness, and that he had not noticed it till it touched him.

Two is company. Grown bolder, he now crawled more fearlessly over the ground until he came to the place where he had buried the Thing. It had taken root and become alive. Out of the soil—no longer barren—a bush had shot up. The naked clay had clothed itself with hair. Grass was growing upon it.

Still the man felt lonely, and out of the clay he shaped

a figure like his own. Then he sat down again upon the ground and waited. Scarcely had the new figure come to life than it took to shoveling up the earth with its arms. It could not keep still. Without pause, on and on it went piling up the soil around, and Tulungersak discovered that this new creature was of quite a different mind from himself, of an excitable, passionate mind. This did not please him. Seizing it, he dragged it to the verge of the abyss and hurled it over. (This creature, so they say, became Tornak, an evil spirit and the father of all such.)

Tulungersak crawled back to the tree that he had planted. Lo and behold! There had come many beside it, tree after tree! A luxuriant wood had sprung up, full of plants. About the roots of the trees the earth had put forth many small flowers. He touched these gently with his hand, felt their shape, smelled their perfume, but could not see them.

He was now seized with a sudden desire to learn more about the earth on which he was standing, on which he was creeping around, with the little sparrow fluttering above. He could not see the bird, but always he heard the "whirr-whirr-whirr" of its wings, and sometimes it perched on his head or hopped down upon his hand. Because he was afraid to stand upright in the dark he kept creeping on all fours, and, finding water all about him, he discovered that he was on an island.

Now he thought: "I would like to know what is in the abyss down there." So he begged the little sparrow to fly down and explore it. Down it flew and was gone a long, long time. When at length it returned, it told him that it had been down to the depths of the world, a land formless and strange, scarcely yet hardened on the surface. He resolved that he, too, would travel to the depths of the world, and begged the little bird to sit down on his knee, so that by feeling it he might find out how it was made and how it could balance itself so lightly upon its wings. Then, groping his way back to the forest, he broke off wing-shaped boughs and fastened them to his shoulders. But while he was flapping the boughs, lo and behold! They suddenly became real wings! Feathers grew from his body, the lump on his forehead turned into a beak, and he was able to fly like the little bird.

Down they dived together to the depths of the world. But just as he took wing the man cried: "Kaok! Kaok!" He had become a big black bird. He called himself Raven.

The place they came from he called the sky, and it was such a distance from there to the depths of the world that he was utterly exhausted when he reached the bottom.

Here everything was bleak and bare. The Raven planted the bottom of the world just as he had done the sky. He flew from place to place with the sparrow, and a wood grew up, tree after tree, with herbs and plants about their roots. This new land the Raven called "earth."

After the earth had become fruitful, the Raven created men. Some say that he made them of clay, just as he had made a figure after his own image up in the sky. But others believe that man's creation was a chance thing, still more wonderful than if he had been made by design.

Father Raven went round and planted herbs and flowers,

and suddenly he spied some pod plants which he had never noticed before. When he took a look at them, one of the pods suddenly burst, and a full grown, well shaped man hopped out! The Raven was so astonished that he threw up his beak and thus became a man himself.

Smilingly he went up to the newcomer and asked, "Who are you? And wherever do you come from?"

"I came from that pod," said the man, pointing to the hole through which he had jumped. "I was weary of lying there, so I kicked a hole and jumped out."

Father Raven laughed heartily at that and answered:

"Aj! Aj! Aj! You're a funny fellow! I've never seen your like!" and he laughed again. "As a matter of fact," he added, "I planted that pod myself, though goodness knows I never dreamed that anyone like you would jump out of it. But the earth we're standing on isn't ready yet. Don't you notice how it quakes? Let's fly over to that hill yonder, it's steady enough there."

Only then did the man notice that the ground he stood on was quaking, and he made haste to quit it with Father Raven.

That was how the first man was made, and Father Raven created many more, men and women too. It is said that all of them, except the first four men, were fashioned out of clay. But the four that came from a pea pod became the ancestors of earth's strongest sons.

Man was now created. But it is said that at first there wasn't much difference between a man and an animal, the one could change into the other. And men walked on their hands, or crawled about on all fours. It was only afterwards that they learned to walk upright on their feet.

At first Father Raven fed men with berries from the plants that he had sown. But what could be gathered from the plants or grubbed up from their roots wasn't enough for men. They had to have more food, and so animals were made.

The Raven made all kinds of animals on the earth, in the air, and in the sea, and he made them of clay, as he had made mankind. He showed them to the men and said that this was to be their food as soon as they had learned to hunt. But that wasn't easy as the earth was quite dark, and eyes were of no use. If men wanted to walk they had to grope about with their hands and find things out by listening.

It was all listening.

Men heard the husky coughing of caribou; they heard the howling of wolves, the grunting of bears, foxes barking, "Kak! Kak! Kak!" In the sea the seal snorted, the walrus wheezed, the whale blew. Birds whistled and sang, insects hummed. Men heard, too, the whispering of the winds, the rustle and murmur of the leaves, and the surging of the surf against the shore.

They were in the midst of a life that they could only perceive through sound. Nothing was to be seen; everywhere people were groping about in darkness, and it was not easy to live.

Then the Raven called the little sparrow to him and said: "You were here before I found myself sitting on the ground.

Maybe you know more than I do. Fly out into the world and find something that can make earth light enough for people to see each other and the land round their houses and the animals they must hunt."

And the little sparrow flew off and stayed away in the darkness until the Raven thought it was never coming back. One couldn't tell day from night: it was all the same. There was no Time, and the Raven didn't know how long the sparrow had been away. At last, however, he heard the whirr of its wings and felt it floating down on him and settling on his hand.

In its beak it bore two pieces of mica wrapped in a leaf, a light piece and a dark piece. These it gave to the Raven.

The Raven broke a little off the light piece and threw it into the air. Immediately a great radiance filled the earth and dazzled everyone. The light was so strong that it was a long time before even the Raven could see.

For the first time men beheld the land on which they lived; they saw the woods, the creatures on earth and in the sea, and the birds in the air; and they rejoiced over the Beauty that surrounded them.

Life became a new and a greater thing for all.

But this blinding radiance was too strong. So the Raven broke a piece off the black mica and threw it up into the air.

Immediately the light was dimmed. Men could see without hurting their eyes, and with the dark mica came night and rest. Light and Darkness were wedded.

Now people were happy. The Raven taught them to build houses in which to find shelter from wind and weather, and he taught them to make kayaks and umiaks and all kinds of fishing gear, so that they could become seafarers and hunt the sea creatures. But men and animals kept increasing, and their island was in danger of becoming too small. Only the sea was big.

Then one day there arose from the sea, just off the people's island, a huge black mass—a vast monster unlike any other animal. The men rowed up to it in umiaks and kayaks and tried to harpoon it; but all the harpoons rattled off its sides —the monster never noticed them!

The Raven saw this hopeless struggle and said to the little sparrow:

"Follow me and hover above this monster while I hunt it from my kayak."

So he rowed out, and while the sparrow was hovering overhead, he killed the monster with a cast of his harpoon.

The men shouted with joy and towed it home to their houses and skinned it. They cut it up into little bits and threw these out into the sea all around. Lo! Out of the ocean grew islands; land shot up near land and the whole became a wide and spacious coast. In this way the mainland was created, and there was enough room on the earth for everybody, men and animals, too.

But when the earth was quite complete, the Raven gathered all the men and said to them:

"I am your father. To me you owe your land and your lives and you must never forget me."

And rising from the ground, he flew up to the sky, where it was still dark. Here he threw out the rest of the white

And rising from the ground, Father Raven flew up to the sky,
where it was still dark.

mica and the light sent its vast flames over the world. Heaven and Earth were created.

In this way was the earth made, and men and animals. But the Raven came first—except for the little sparrow.

Told by Apákag from Noatak River.

THE EARTH'S ISLANDS BECOME MAINLAND, AND MEN HUNT MAMMOTHS

THE earth has not always been as it is now, nor have the animals which we hunt. Our first forefathers hunted large game which is no longer to be found. The birds, too, have altered, for men can remember that they were once heavy and slow. That was in the days when men walked on their hands.

Everything is different now, earth, animals, and men. Nowadays everything living can be killed with our weapons, and we hear with astonishment of all the giant animals which in old days were dangerous to hunters; for their size made them invulnerable.

There was a time when there was no mainland. All land seemed crushed into scattered fragments. The vast plains which are now watered by rivers rich in fish were not to be found. Men lived on high islands that were washed by the sea. Even then men were skillful whalers, and many whales were towed in. The cut-up blubber had to be carried to the mountains, where men had their tents and houses, for fear of the big waves. That is why the bones of whales are often to be found a long way from the sea and far up the mountains.

The first lands that were inhabited were the uplands by Umiat, Uivfagtait, and other hills up in the higher reaches of Colville River. There were also, of course, people on the high mountains around Point Hope and in behind Kotzebue Sound. Not until after the time when Father Raven harpooned a sea animal that floated on the crest of the waters, which had neither beginning nor end, was the great mainland created. Then the mountains became connected by lowland, and the earth grew bigger. Therefore all lowland is new land.

Old *shamans* relate also that when the mainland was first created it was still bigger than it is now, and a man could walk from Cape Prince of Wales over Diomedes Islands to Nuvung, right across Bering Strait to the big settlement by East Cape. All that remains now are the shoals that jut out into the sea from the farthest strips of the lagoons.

The lands in Bering Strait that were first connected with each other were the two high islands, Big and Little Diomedes. A low tongue of land lay between them, but later an earthquake sundered them. The ribs of whales from the sunken habitations could be seen long after, sticking up from the sea. Of this it is related:

There was once a young man who had caught a little baby

seal and put it into his kayak behind the manhole in order
to bring it home alive. But the baby seal, terrified, scratched
him in the back during the whole journey to the settlement.
There were no ice floes where the kayak man could lie to
and come out of his kayak. And although he hurried for all
he was worth, the seal had scratched such deep holes in his
back that he died just as he reached land. His mother, who
thus lost her only son, revenged herself by flaying the skin
from the living seal, and putting the "naked" animal back
into the water. But the young seal took revenge too. It
raised an earthquake so violent that the spit of land with
the entire settlement sank into the sea. In this way arose
the two islands, Big and Little Diomedes.

All this shows how old the earth is; and no one therefore
can wonder that there was once game that we no longer
know.

The most prodigious of all animals was the one we call
kilivfak, the mammoth. All over the tundras its skeletons
lie, and we marvel at the enormous size of its bones. So immense could its tusks be that a single man had difficulty in
carrying even one of them. They were of fine ivory, even
better than walrus tusk. When we find the tusk of a mammoth, we make weapons out of it, or we carve drinking horns
which are far bigger and handsomer than those made of the
horn of the musk ox. Everything that is made of mammoth
tusk has the protective power of an amulet.

These great animals we find now deep down in the ground,
and it is remarkable that all that our forefathers relate con-
cerning them bears out the tradition of their immense

strength which enabled them to dive down in places where there were no caves or holes whenever they were tired of walking above ground.

We have two stories about the hunting of mammoths.

There was once a man who was out hunting. He was spying for game when he caught sight of something that ripped up the surface of the ground. It was far inland and yet it looked like a sea creature cleaving the surface of the waters, so easily did it toss the soil about. The man stared and stared at the moving clods, until out came the tusks of a mammoth; that was what was piercing the crust of the tundras. So the man stretched his bow and shot an arrow into the ground a little bit behind and underneath the place which the tusks rooted up. He did no more. Then he went home and lay down to sleep. Next morning he started off again, refreshed and in good spirits, and went back to the same place. And there on top of the ground lay a huge, huge animal, a mammoth that had fallen over on its knees and died of its wound.

The other tale we remember likewise deals with a man who was out hunting He was going down through a mountain gorge when he suddenly spied a mammoth that shot up through the ground. Right on its heels leapt a dog that pursued it, and after the dog came a man, who sprang in the mammoth's footprints way down in the ground, armed only with a knife. The whole thing seemed like a vision, it was so incredible. But just as soon as they dived up they vanished again in the earth, the mammoth and the dog and the man who followed in its traces. They appeared and disappeared like a flying landslide or a rolling stone upon a mountain slope. And they came to the surface no more.

We who are living now think that these are remarkable tales, but when we find bones or tusks deep down in the earth and compare them with parts of the skeletons of the land animals we now hunt, we understand that the tales are not necessarily untrue, even if they do seem incredible. For in those days there were many things in nature which were far, far more overwhelming than those we are now accustomed to see.

Told by Sagluaq.

Right on its heels leapt a dog that pursued it, and after the dog
came a man

THE FOUR COMRADES WHO WANTED
TO TRAVEL ROUND THE WORLD

THERE was once a big settlement near the sea. Here lived many men who hunted caribou far inland, but the greater part of the year they hunted on the sea. They had no chieftain, no one to guide them. Every evening they gathered together in the feast hall, and all the young people enjoyed themselves.

One evening, when, as usual, there was song and dance, some of the young men stepped forward and said:

"We will travel round the world; we will see what it is like. We wish to meet other people. We wish to find material for tales and songs. Young people ought to experience wonderful things before they grow old."

So out they set, the four young men. They went along the seashore, for they wanted to travel round the whole earth. When they had traveled for two nights and three days, they suddenly saw a house before them, quite an ordinary house, but there were no people outside, and they went into the hall, and there they went on and on. The world had all at once disappeared for them; there was no sky, no sea, and no earth; they were walking in a passage which had no end. Gradually such a long time passed that the young men aged. They had only down on their chins when they set out; now they had regular beards. The beards grew long and turned gray, and still the men hadn't come more than halfway into the house. They grew gray-haired and wrinkled; their legs grew weak, and they walked with sticks. At last one of them collapsed entirely. He sank down and breathed his last, and the others had to abandon him and go on. Then another had to give up, and another died of old age, and the only one who was left of the four young men crawled on alone, bent with years and age. Then he turned about, found the way out of the house, and went back to his dwelling. He recognized his country and was filled with gladness. Folk came to meet him, but instead of welcoming him back they cried:

"A stranger! A stranger!"

Nobody recognized him; all his comrades were dead.

When they gathered in the feast hall in the evening he was at last recognized by a man who had grown so old that he never left the feast hall; he lived there night and day, as is the custom when old men have become lonely and have no relatives. This man now told his neighbors that as a child he had heard tell how four young men had set out to travel round the world, but they had never returned. At these words the old world wanderer stood up, stepped out on the floor, and related:

"We set out to go round the world; but we had only traveled two nights and three days when we entered a house that seemed endless. Air and sea and sky had vanished from us, and in order not to become quite lost we had to go round and round and round along what we took to be the walls of the house. We could not turn back, and we went on and continued to go on. We grew beards, our hair grew white, our skin grew wrinkled, and my comrades died of age. I am the only one to return. And all that I can tell is that the earth is enormous and that it is round. The earth is round like the inside of an *igdlo.*"

And when the old man had told this he fell to the ground and died.

So huge, so enormous is the earth.

Told by Apákag.

THE CHILD FROM THE SEA

OUT in the big sound (Bering Strait) lie two islands not far from each other; they are called Imarlik and Ingaglik (Big and Little Diomedes). Here lived two chieftains, each on his island, two brothers. Each had a married daughter, but the chief's daughter from Ingaglik had no child, and people always talked about it, saying, "Why haven't you a child?" At last she became distressed and grew moody and went about in silence. She had no brothers who could comfort her, no one she could confide in, and she went about alone with her great sorrow. Six years passed, yet she gave birth to no child. Then, in the spring, while everyone else was out whaling, a child was born.

But what was this? It was no proper child. Its skin was like a seal's, all speckled like the skin of a little fjord seal, and the woman became ashamed and took her child and laid it on the drying-rack over the lamp. Here she kept it hidden that none might see it. But one day her parents came on a visit; they discovered that something lay on the drying-rack over the lamp, where the air was nice and warm, and they asked her what it was. The girl would not tell them, but the parents continued to urge her, and at last she had to confess that she had had a child which was no proper human being. The parents at once wanted to see it. "Ah! Do let us see it," they cried. But the girl answered: "I won't let you see it. I am ashamed." The child remained lying on the drying-rack, and nobody was allowed to see it.

But one day when the girl was outside, she heard a sound like an explosion within the house. She was cooking bearded seal meat for her parents, when the fire suddenly flared up, and the flames roared high in the air. At the same moment an explosion came from inside the house, and she heard her child cry, "Mother! Mother!" She hastened into the house and found both parents dead upon the floor. They had seen the child.

One day her husband came home from the whale-fishing, and he came to meet her, calling gladly:

"Is it true what they say, that I have a son—a son?"

The wife immediately grew distressed and told him what had happened. It was no ordinary child, it was no proper human being, the child was like a little fjord seal; he must never set eyes on it. And now she told him about the parents who were dead because they would not listen, but managed to see the child while she herself was out.

The mother tended her child quite alone and sometimes

carried it on her back, covered up and hidden, so that none
should see it. But one day when she had to cook meat for
her husband at the fireplace outside the house, the same
thing happened that had happened once before. The fire
flared violently, the flames shot out, and at the same moment
she heard an explosion and rushed into the house. "Mother!
Mother!" cried the child, and when she came in the husband
lay dead upon the floor. He had seen his child. And the poor
woman, who was beside herself with sorrow and shame, had
to bury her husband just as she had buried her parents.

Now it became widely reported that there was a woman
who had a child the sight of whom caused people to die, and
as the timidity of men is nearly always less great than their
curiosity, there were many who came to see the child. No one
believed that people spoke the truth about it. But the child's
mother held them off, saying: "No one shall see my child.
My parents died of it, my husband died of it. No more
people shall die from seeing my child."

Yet nearly every time the young people had been playing
ball, they came past the house on their way home and
wanted to see the child. One evening their curiosity was so
great that the woman was not strong enough to hold back
the most insistent; they forced their way into the house and
saw the child, and all dropped down dead upon the floor.

The young wife grieved over the fate she had met, and
over the child she had borne and the curse that hung over it.
At last she no longer dared to lie down and rest in her dwelling, but went to the mountains and kept herself hidden.
One spring, when the ice stretched over the mainland, she

fled over the big strait and continued farther along the coast and into the country, merely to get away from people and live in solitude.

One day, however, she ran into people, and when they saw her they went to meet her, crying:

"Where do you come from? We had no idea there were people in the neighborhood. Stay with us, we are so lonely."

They gave her food, and it wasn't long before they wanted to see her child. In vain did she tell them of the curse that hung over the child; the people among whom she found herself were incredulous, as people usually are. They insisted on seeing the child; and they fared no better than all the others, but fell to the ground and died at once.

Then the young woman left the place and went sadly on. Gladly would she have lived in a settlement with other people, but she dared not. She went farther inland, and wore out her footgear, and was often hungry. She had to satisfy herself by eating the berries of the earth, and she grew lean and famished; she had no milk for her child, and it did not grow, and cried for hunger.

But one day, when she saw a flock of caribou, she said to the child: "You must not be seen by men or women; let the animals see you, let the caribou herd see you." And she lifted the child up and showed it to the animals; and all the caribou fell down and died. So they obtained meat, skin, and clothing. Then they grew strong and fat, and went farther across the country.

One day they came to a house. There were no people to be seen, but outside the house there was a large meat gibbet filled with caribou meat. She went into the house; here she saw only men's clothing, no women's garments. She remained there the whole day without food. When evening came she heard a voice outside:

"Ej! Ej! Where do you come from to me, who live alone here without help?" In came a young man, and it wasn't long before the two became man and wife. But now it happened, as always before, that the young man wanted to see her child.

"You will die," said the wife, "if you see my child."

But the man did not believe her and answered:

"I don't care to live if I can't see your child." So he raised the flap of the *amaut* and peeped in at the child. Immediately a mighty flame shot up, an explosion was heard, an avalanche of stones wiped out the house, and when the woman came to herself, she sat on the bare ground alone with her child.

Again she went on in distress. Never could she be with other people, however great her longing was, because all people were incredulous and inquisitive and would not believe what she said. She went over a mountain ridge, up to the top, and there she sat down and looked out over a great sea with many, many houses along the coast. She burst into tears; all these houses, all these people, and yet she dared not go down there! Suddenly the child moved and said:

"Mother, why didn't you say to your parents: 'Come again?' Then they would have revived." That was the child's word, and suddenly he began to grow; he became a proper boy and wanted to get out of the *amaut*.

"Mother! Mother! Now you can see me," said the boy. And there he stood, hard featured and ugly, almost without nose, with a flat face just like the head of a little fjord seal. And he said: "You shall call me Lard" (Qaluneq).

They went down together to the houses. There stood house after house, a big settlement with many people. Here dwelt two great chieftains. The older was married, the younger unmarried. They lived in plenty and ate only caribou and whale meat. Before long, the young chief married the woman with the ugly child. The child grew up quickly and was now almost like an ordinary human being.

The year passed. The two chieftains' wives were with child, and each bore a son. But one day, when little Lard was playing with the older chief's half-grown son, it chanced that they began to squabble:

"You are so ugly that you don't look like a human creature," said the chief's son.

Lard became angry and cried:

"Turn round and look me straight in the face."

At the same moment a flame shot out, an explosion was heard, and the chief's son fell to the ground, dead.

Lard's mother was unhappy, and she begged everybody in the settlement never on any account to tease her son, because he was no ordinary human being. He was dangerous: one might die by looking at him. And after that folk were cautious.

Meanwhile Lard's little brother grew up, and they always played together, these two. Years passed, and they became half-grown boys. When they were hunting ptarmigan it

might happen that Lard said to his half brother: "Turn
your back!" Then he just looked at the ptarmigan and they
all lay dead on the ground at one and the same moment.
In this way they hunted together, not only caribou, but all
kinds of game. At last they reached young manhood and
were big enough to go whaling. So they hunted whale together and always in such a way that Lard sat in the bow
of his brother's skin boat and let the whales see him, while
all the others hid. In this way the brothers caught many
whales.

Spring came, and the two brothers went inland to hunt
caribou. One day they saw a giant bird of the kind that is
called mitervik, and that is so big that it can hunt both
caribou and whales. When they saw it, Lard said to his
brother: "Lie down!" And he showed himself to the giant
fowl. A flame, an explosion, and the giant bird was dead.
They stripped off its skin with feet, head, and wings attached,
and dried it carefully; then they softened it and hid it in the
place where they had caught the bird.

From here they continued their way into the woods and
hunted caribou and bear for a time, and when the spring
again began to thaw the ground, they returned to the place
where they had hidden the giant bird's skin. Here Lard now
attired himself in the skin while singing a magic song.

Immediately he could soar high toward the sky and fly
over all the country. And from this time on he always followed the chase in the giant bird's skin and always came
back with caribou in his mighty claws.

Lard was always with his brother, and they always hunted

together. He made himself a umiak and became a chief in the settlement.

One day his half brother teased him, saying to him:

"You are so ugly that you can never be married. There is no girl that would have a husband with such a head without a nose, with a flat face like that of a little fjord seal."

Lard became silent, but did his brother no harm. He was silent all winter and hardly ever ate anything. He had now hunted all kinds of animals, and one day he said to his brother:

"There is still an animal I want to hunt: such an animal has never hitherto been hunted, and that is why I am silent."

"I'll come too, you won't survive the hunt. I am going out to hunt the world's largest animals; they are called *qernerit* —'the Big Black Ones' and if they kill you I will die also."

But the brother would not give in, and at last Lard had to take him along. They went across the country, far, far over mountains, until they came to a lake that was so big that it looked like the sea. High steep mountains upon whose slopes stones lay piled surrounded it and amid these stones they slowly passed the lake. Soon after, they came to a second, yet larger, lake, in the middle of which stood an island, and another, and still another, and even a fourth—four big, dark islands. Suddenly one of them moved; it raised itself and began to wade towards land. What had seemed to be islands were *kilivfak*, the big black mammoths. They had a long hunting finger in the snout, and one of them carried a caribou.

Lard had fashioned himself a harpoon from a tree trunk,

with a huge flint at the point. He had also cut a harpoon for his brother, and now, when he saw the nozzled animal, he whispered to him: "Wait here on the shore while I attack!" And he covered himself with a little sealskin pelt, the dress his mother had put on him when he was born; now he used magic and made it big enough to fit him, and then he jumped into the lake, and disappeared in its depths with his spear in his hand. The brother saw only a whirlpool when the animal with the snout was attacked, a whirlpool of boiling water, a rain of stones, a cataclysm of breakers, and all the land darkened under a rain of stones. The animal reached the shore with broken hunting finger and fell dead. The fine weather returned, and Lard was again merry as before.

"That was certainly an animal worth killing," was all that he said.

After that they went home together and hunted whale. Lard put on his giant bird's shape and attacked the whales from the air, and he took them in his claws and lifted them up out of the water, sprawling like trout, and thus he came flying home with them.

One day Lard said to his brother:

"To-day I am going to fly alone, you must not come with me." And he put on his bird shape and rose into the air, crossed over the mountains and searched for strange dwellings. At last he found what he sought; it was a beautiful young woman, daughter of a chief.

"If she would only go alone to the mountains another day!" he thought, and so flew home. Next day he flew out

What had seemed to be islands were big black mammoths.

again, and lo! the woman had done exactly what he wanted. She was alone, and he bore down on her, seized her, and flew home with her.

So did Lard get himself a wife.

Two winters passed, and they decided to visit the girl's parents. A umiak was made, a wonderful boat covered with selected skins of bearded seal, and in this they sailed to the land of the chief, who still lamented the loss of his daughter and had never ceased looking for her. But scarcely had he set eyes on his daughter and her husband than he burst into tears and said:

"What ugly wretch is that you have married? Is that a husband for you, such a fright as that?"

But the daughter answered:

"Don't talk like that. My husband is a chieftain above all other chieftains. Say nothing about him until you know him better."

Lard settled down with his father-in-law and hunted as usual. There was an abundance of meat, and seldom did he come home without caribou or whale in his talons. His wife bore a son, a big boy, who gave promise of being some day just as powerful a man and a hunter as his father. After a while they traveled back to their old dwelling, but not until Lard had caught two whales for his father-in-law.

But after Lard had a son he was no longer himself. He grew more and more silent; and no one understood this, for now that he had carried on his race they all thought that he had cause for nothing but gladness.

One day he went to his mother and said:

"Mother, give me the clothes of my childhood. I must now fare to my own folk. I was born among men and a son has been born to me who will have strong descendants. Now it is time that I should return to my own folk, my own race, who do not live here on earth."

With these words Lard gave the giant bird's skin to his son and took his leave. All the men came out to see him for the last time, and without a word Lard turned towards the ocean, went out on the ice and stopped at a little crack near the open sea. Here he turned round and cried:

"Now I return home! Now I fare forth into the deep!" And he vanished in the ice and was gone. Nobody knew where he had come from, and nobody knew whither he went. His old mother, his wife, and all his house mates stood and stared silently towards the place where he had vanished.

He was the child from the sea.

Told by Apákag.

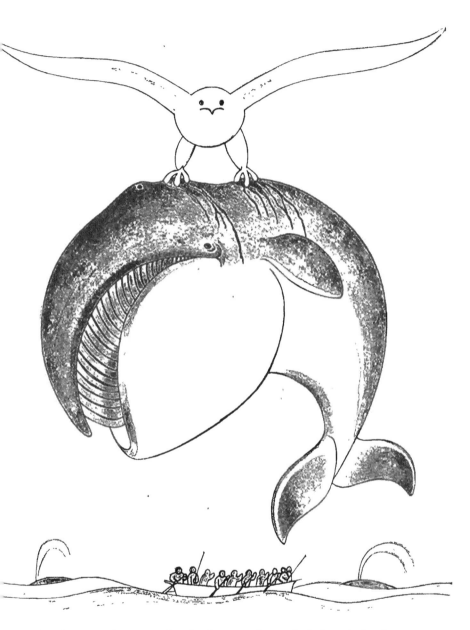

Lard put on his giant bird's shape and attacked the whales from
the air

THE MOST BEAUTIFUL BIRD AND THE LOVELIEST WOMAN

ONCE there lived many people at the mouth of a big river; they had a chief who every year rowed the men out to sea in his skin boat, and all hunted for seals together.

At the same settlement there lived a childless couple; the man used to go on the sea with the others, but he was no great hunter, and often there was no meat in his house.

One spring, when the ice began to break up and the snow had vanished from the mountain sides, the man and his wife went out to gather roots, for they could get nothing else to eat. They were standing together grubbing about in the ground when suddenly they heard a child weeping. The woman immediately began looking about among the tussocks and found a little child near a tree just on the outskirts of a wood.

It was a boy, and you may imagine that they rejoiced over

such a find. The woman took the boy in her arms and carried him home. For a long time they made vain inquiry regarding the parents, but found no mother to the child. At last they adopted him as their own. He was a fine boy who grew up quickly, but he was smaller than other children. They gave him the name of Migssorqhe, but most persons called him merely "Tussock-child."

Now it happened at the settlement that some hunters who were out on the chase disappeared; they never returned from hunting, and one day Tussock-child said to his mother:

"Mother, I want to go and look for all the men who disappear. If only I could get a little bow and an arrow!" And he got a bow and an arrow and went off in the direction where the men used to hunt. Far inland he caught sight of remarkable tracks and followed them. And before long he saw an animal he had never met before on his expeditions, a wild and dangerous animal; but this boy, who was no ordinary mortal, crept near it and shot it with his little bow, and after that no hunter ever was missing. This was Tussock-child's first exploit as a half-grown youth. He grew up and became a young man, and everyone was very fond of him.

One day strangers came to the settlement, four young men with long thin staves in their hands. In the evening these young men told at the feast hall that they had come for Tussock-child; they came from his older brother, who had invited him for a visit, but, they added, he might only come if he could bring with him the bird Qinersinaituaq, a remarkable bird which was so beautiful that none could bear to look at it. Everyone who saw it opened his eyes so wide with astonishment that they burst; the human eye could not endure the sight of it. Therefore the bird was called Qinersinaituaq, which means, "The one that cannot be looked upon."

Tussock-child was not afraid. He asked the messengers to wait and told them that he would surely find the bird. Many young men joined company with him when he began to search, and they went inland and hunted everywhere, but they found no bird so beautiful that their eyes could not endure the sight of it. At last Tussock-child grew silent. He ate nothing and became thin and lean. In vain people offered him food and drink; he always answered:

"I will not eat nor drink before I have found the bird I am looking for."

At last he called his mother and said:

"Mother, you must know where the bird dwells."

"That I do," answered the mother, "but it will kill you; you will stare the eyes out of your head if you see it. Therefore I won't tell you."

"Now, Mother, since I am to die at all events, let me rather die from seeing the bird. If I don't succeed I shall perish of hunger anyway."

Then the mother told him to go far, far inland. Here he would see a mountain that was easy to find, for it towered up over all the others; behind this high, steep mountain, far from mankind, lived the world's most beautiful bird.

Then Tussock-child was happy; he ate and drank and

soon became himself again. As soon as he had regained his full powers, he hastened inland and began looking for the world's highest mountain. He found it, climbed it, and came down on the other side into a valley. Through the valley ran a big, big river, surrounded by dense woods. Here he hid amid the trees, and before long he saw a great bird come sailing through the air, a bird so wonderful that he could never have imagined anything so lovely. Hastily he took aim without daring to look at it closely, and shot it down with his arrow. The bird fell close beside him, and now he saw that its many brilliant colors were so dazzling that they blinded the eyes. When one looked at them, one's eyelids began to quiver; the skin around the eyes expanded; the eyes could not endure the many beautiful colors. He flayed it and took it home with him, but took good heed to show it to no one in the settlement.

Tussock-child was a remarkable young man. It seemed as if he knew beforehand what was going to happen, and one day he went out and shot an owl. Nobody knew what he was going to do with the owl. He was now quite his old lively self, and one day he said to the four young men who had come from his brother that he was now ready to accompany them. They set off and went far, far inland, far from all men's dwellings, and they came to a huge stake, looking like a tree-trunk without any end; it stood like a column that went from earth right up to the sky. Here the messengers suddenly began to soar. They rose from the ground, and Tussock-child went with them. They soared round and round the column and rose higher and higher in the air, until the earth was almost lost sight of. High up in the air they came to a hole that went right into the sky. They slipped through this and now stood in Skyland, a great and beautiful country where there dwelt many people. Here they were well received and regaled with all kinds of choice meats. When they had eaten and all were satisfied, Tussock-child's brother stepped forward in the feast hall and said:

"I asked you to come, but only if you could kill the bird none can bear to look upon. Have you done so?"

Immediately Tussock-child took out the skin of the bird and laid it on the ground, and everyone had to shut his eyes, none could endure the brilliant colors; all the corners of their eyes quivered. Tussock-child hastened to conceal the bird skin and laid out in its place the skin of the owl he had shot, and the folk rested their eyes on the owl skin, which was without strong colors, and the brother, who had been on the point of fainting, said, as soon as he had recovered: "An amazing thing have you shown us, and a wonderful deed did you perform when you killed the bird which I myself have hunted in vain. You are a great man and I will go back with you to your dwelling."

But now Tussock-child spoke and said:

"You shall accompany me to my dwelling, but not until you have found a woman who is so beautiful that none can bear to look upon her."

To this the brother agreed, and at once began to search, just as Tussock-child had searched for birds; but he could not find any woman who was so beautiful that none could bear to look at her. At last he became taciturn and lost interest in life, ate nothing, and drank nothing. One day he called his mother to him and said:

"Mother, you know where there lives a woman who is so lovely that none can bear to look upon her."

"That I do," answered the mother, "but you will die if you see her."

"If I remain at home, I shall die of hunger," answered the son. And so his mother told him where he must go. He must go right over the highest back of a mighty mountain chain which was to be found up in Skyland, and when he had crossed it, he must look for a lake, and there he would find the world's loveliest woman.

It was spring. The snow had melted from the sunny sides of the mountains, and the man went overland to climb the great mountain chain at its highest point. On the other side of the mountains he saw a lake. Here he caught sight of four women who waded out into the water near the shore. He went down to the lake, and, covered by the stones and brushwood on the shore, he sneaked unseen over to the place where the four bathers had hidden their garments. As soon as he had seized their clothing he made his presence known, and the four women screamed from fear and came running up to him.

"Our clothes! Our clothes!" they shouted, and the man looked at them and noticed that one of them was so lovely that he had to shut his eyes; she blinded him, he dared not look at her. He gave the other three their garments, but kept the beautiful woman with him, taking her home in a chest. He was afraid that his neighbors would die if they saw her.

Thereupon he sent festal messengers to his brother, as men are wont to do when great tidings are to be brought from dwelling to dwelling. Young men in new garments, with long thin staves in their hands, were sent out. They were to announce to Tussock-child that his brother was coming to him, and the brother appeared and a big banquet was held, where the guests were given all kinds of good food to eat. When the meal was over and all were still assembled in the feast hall, Tussock-child spoke and said to his brother:

"You required me to slay the world's most beautiful bird before I should visit you, and I did it. In return I asked you to bring me the world's most beautiful woman. Have you brought her with you?"

The brother now carried a chest into the hall, and out of this chest sprang a young and lovely woman. It was as if a great light, warm and blinding, had been released in the feast hall.

All lowered their gaze, and the corners of their eyes quivered. The only one who could bear to look at her was Tussock-child, and so he took the world's most beautiful woman for his wife and afterwards became a mighty man upon the earth.

Who Tussock-child was nobody ever learned. He was found near a tuft under a tree, but as he had a brother in Skyland it has been supposed that he, too, belonged to the Sky Folk. All we know is that he lived his life upon earth, and that he and his descendants gave new strength and courage to Humanity.

Told by Apákag.

THE GIRL ALARANA AND HER BROTHER, WHO WERE EATEN BY WOLVES AND AFTERWARDS TURNED INTO CARIBOU

ONCE a famine broke out at Point Barrow, and all the people starved to death, except two of one family, the girl Alarana and her little brother Aligunaluk. Since no others were left alive, they departed and wandered inland to try to join the caribou hunters, who had gone up the river Kulugjuaq. But on their way they were suddenly surrounded by a pack of wolves that tore them to pieces and ate them.

Among the beasts there was an old she-wolf that asked all the young wolves to pay great heed that no bones should be bitten through or crushed. It was in the days when people were at one time men, and at another, animals, and so it was in this case. As soon as the wolves had eaten the brother and sister, they became men, and now it was an old woman who asked to have the human bones brought into the house.

The wolf-people lived in a big fine house, and it was not

wolves alone who had their abode there. There were also
guests on the side-bunk, and these guests were a raven and
a sea gull, a white fox and a red fox. But for the time being
these also wore the shapes of men.

As soon as Alarana's and her brother's bones were brought
into the house, the old woman, who understood witchcraft,
went out and fetched two caribou skins, the skins of a young
cow and a little bull calf. These two skins she spread out on
the floor and placed the brother's and sister's bones on
them, the head first and then all the remaining bones in their
places. Then she covered all the bones with the sewed-
together guts of walrus and sang a magic song over them,
while walking round the bones in the same direction as the
sun in the sky. It was not long before Alarana's bones were
joined and began to move; but her little brother would not
come to life. So the old woman sang the magic song again,
and now Alarana sat up, but still her little brother did not
stir.

"Some of the boy's bones must have been forgotten," said
the old woman.

"Kak-kak-ka," was heard immediately, and out of the
house sprang the white fox and the red fox, and it was not
long before they came back with the boy's loin-bones that
had been lost in the snow.

Again the old woman said charms over the bones, and
now both brother and sister regained their human shape and
awakened to life, Alarana in a fine dress of a young caribou
cow's skin, her brother in the skin of a quite young bull
calf. They were assigned a place at the back of the *briks,* and

there they lay during the day, but at night they slept with the old woman who had called them to life. At the end of four days the little brother was allowed to go out, for four days is the death tabu which is appointed for men and boys; but at night he had to join his sister, who was not yet allowed to leave the house. The boy wept and did not want to come back, and his sister had to reason with him through the window. Not until the day after, did she, also, receive permission to go out, for then the death tabu for women had run its course. In the evening they took part in a great banquet consisting of caribou, whale and walrus; such a banquet was formerly celebrated whenever dead men were called to life; and the next day they were permitted to travel wherever they liked.

The brother and sister went inland, following a river. Towards evening they caught sight of a big herd of caribou that were grazing on a slope, and they went up to them without seeking any cover, and without thinking that perhaps they might scare the animals away. But, lo, the animals paid no attention whatever to them, nor were they afraid of the animals, and Alarana and her brother mingled fearlessly with the herd. Only then did they discover that they were no longer men, but that the old she-wolf had charmed their garments in such a way that they were now caribou among caribou. They were hungry and at once sought their way to a cow, who was shovelling the snow away with her forefeet so that the moss showed. Here they got leave to eat the remnants, and behold! strange as it may seem, the moss was not moss when they had it in their mouths, but it was guts and whaleskin and meat and all other kinds of food that tasted good.

Alarana and her brother now remained with the caribou. They soon discovered that their comrades slept only very little during the night, and, when awake, ate almost continuously, at the same time watching the surrounding country sharply, for fear of being surprised by enemies. Every morning, at the very earliest dawn, they set off to seek for other grazing places. But the snow was deep, and Alarana and her brother could not keep up with them to begin with; they had to content themselves with following in the others' tracks as well as they could. Sometimes they could not catch up with the others before evening set in. But they always went up to one of the cows, still feeling like children who needed a mother, and they ate what the caribou cow left, which was all they needed.

"How do you manage to run so quickly through the deep snow?" Alarana asked one day.

"Because we always run with our heads well up, so that our eyes can scan the horizon," answered the cow.

Again a night passed with eating and watching and a very short sleep, which was often interrupted, and at the earliest dawn the entire herd was again on the road to the next grazing place. This time Alarana and her brother arched their heads in the same way as the rest of the herd, and they ran with the same lift of neck and shoulder as the other animals and now found it easy to keep up. Thus little by little they learned the caribous' customs; and they learned to shovel the snow away with their forefeet, so that they could find moss themselves, moss which, as soon as it entered their mouths, always became delicious food for man.

One day, while grazing together with the rest of the herd, they heard a creaking in the snow, and lo! .a man came walking toward them, the first man they had seen since they became caribou. The girl immediately sang a magic song:

> *"May the man over there*
> *Stumble upon his snowshoes,*
> *Stumble upon his creaking snowshoes,*
> *And may I myself grow so small*
> *That the man's arrow*
> *May shoot past my body."*

This song afterwards became a very effective magic song for caribou hunters who wish booty; for the man stood still and listened to the words, and meanwhile Alarana and her brother detached themselves from the herd and saved themselves in the depths of the wood. They were now caribou and had thoroughly acquired the habits of caribou. They walked and ate, ate and walked, always on the alert, resting only seldom: such was their life.

In autumn they came to a big enclosure with snares, where men were in the habit of trapping caribou, but they knew the ruse of humans and avoided it by going outside of all the pales to which the snares were fastened. Here they found the carcass of a ptarmigan full of maggots. The bird had

been surprised by a herd of fleeing caribou and been tram-
pled to death. But the girl lifted up the carcass and sang
another magic song:

> *"Moist art thou, unhappy carcass,*
> *Maggot-eaten little ptarmigan."*

And lo! instantly the ptarmigan came to life and flew
away, cackling. And it is said that since then these words
also became an active and life-giving magic song among men.

On went the brother and sister, a young cow and a little
bull calf, leaping merrily about. After a while they came to a
river where they found a stone, round and shining because
many stone weapons had been whetted on it. Again the girl
sang a song, a magic grinding song:

> *"This little stone*
> *Is round and shining*
> *From knives of slate*
> *That are whetted against it.*
> *Hard stone, smooth stone,*
> *Round and shining."*

This song, too, was remembered, and afterwards became
among men a good magic song for knife grinders.

On they went, on and on, across country or swimming
across lakes and wading through rivers, always on the alert,
always resting little but grazing much.

One day they came to a wood, a big, thick wood. A storm

was blowing, and the trees on the edge of the wood swayed, whistling and sobbing to and fro in the wind. The two caribou believed that the trees were alive, and they were frightened, but again the sister sang a magic song:

"Darkly whisper
The trees of the woodland;
Sighing, they sway
And make us afraid."

Immediately Alarana and her brother were reassured. Afraid no longer, they sprang gladly into the depths of the woodland; but since then the song has become a powerful incantation against fear in the forests.

The brother and sister wandered on and on as caribou, pausing only for a moment now and then to snatch at the luxuriant moss. The sun had begun to give warmth, the snow was melting, the ice of the streams was breaking up, and the meadows were growing green. Summer arrived. But no men had they seen since they met the hunter whom they tricked with a magic song. The country was vast, and men were few.

One day they caught sight, on the top of a mountain ridge, of a man who waved his arms, and howled like a wolf; they went nearer and saw another man, then still more appeared. They were hunters who howled like wolves, yet the cry did not sound exactly like that of a wolf. These men were out to drive caribou down to a swimming place where kayak men were lying in wait with their harpoons. The brother and sister stopped and looked at them, remembering the days when they, too, took part in driving animals down to a river. While they were thinking of this, suddenly a big herd, fleeing before shouting men, swept them along and drove them down towards the river. They ran in front of the herd, and before long they saw something gleaming ahead of them. It was the river where the kayaks were waiting. They ran down to it and swam across, while all the other animals swung round and turned back to the depths of the forest. Brother and sister saw men lying in wait in their kayaks with their sharp javelins ready to throw, but they were waiting for the big herd and did not attack the two single caribou. So it came to pass that the latter crossed the river unharmed, sprang over the bank on the other side, and hid in a wood where no one pursued them. From this place they heard these words:

"Two caribou separated themselves from the herd and swam across, while all the others turned into the wood again and escaped. We thought the whole herd would jump into the river, and so we let the two slip away."

The next day the brother and sister ran again into the wood to the other caribou, and the same thing happened. The caribou would not take to the river, and the hunters caught no animals, but every evening Alarana stole so close to the camp of the hunters that she could hear them talking. She pined for human speech, and now when she heard it she began to long still more for the dwellings of men. She was seized with a desire to visit them and ran, with her brother, into the depths of the wood and shed her outer coat. Also the brother cast off his coat, and on the ground lay the two wet caribou skins. The brother and sister were again human beings, and as such they visited the settlement.

There were many tents and many people, and all welcomed the strangers. The men said that they had been unlucky with their hunting and could not induce the caribou to jump into the river where the kayaks could pursue them. Then the sister promised to pronounce an incantation and thus obtain prey for them. At once she set about making her preparations. She had the men drag together huge piles of wood from the forest, which was stacked at the settlement, whereupon a great pyre was lighted. The tree trunks were set up in such a way as to form an opening in the middle, which led to the crackling fire of the twigs. Alarana decorated her head with an eagle's feather, as men are wont to do at a sacrificial feast, and when the fire flamed highest she sang her incantation and sprang through the opening into the fire. For a long time she seemed lost in the flames, but after a while the eagle's feather was seen rising slowly, very slowly, from the fire, without a single bit of it having been singed. Next came the girl's head. She too rose slowly from the pyre, and now came quietly forward towards all the men and women of the place, who stood around as spectators.

Alarana had shown to the evil spirits of earth and air her strength and power; and standing in the fire she had compelled them to give the beasts of the chase freedom so that men might have good hunting. She herself was a human being and fond of her race, so she made only one stipulation for the settlement's successful hunting. One solitary caribou had she marked during her vision, and it must be reserved for her when it swam over the river; no one else must get it.

The next day all went hunting as usual, some driving caribou from the woods and down towards the river, others waiting with their kayaks at the swimming place. The forest swarmed with caribou and a mighty herd came leaping out of the thicket. This time they did not turn round, but all swam out into the current. Thus, the kayaks surprised them, and the men got such rich booty that they had to put off skinning the animals till the next day.

But when the animals came leaping out from the wood and set their course towards the river, a solitary caribou had been clearly seen distinguished from the herd. It had shining white hair on its belly and halfway up its flanks, and it did not resemble the others.

"That handsome caribou," said the girl, "is the one I noticed when I stood in the fire, and it is mine."

Next day they went down to the banks of the river to flay the animals. But now there was a young man who would not have any other caribou than the one that was to fall to the girl. Some men are like that. In a strange way and without reason they will desire the very thing they must not have, and thus stand in the way of their own good fortune and that of others. All tried to reason with him, some threatened him, but nothing availed. The young man kept the caribou, and Alarana would have no other.

The same night sister and brother returned to the forest, and here they became caribou again, fleeing shyly from the places where men had their tenting grounds. Since that day nothing more has ever been heard of the brother and sister who were sometimes caribou and sometimes men. But the hunters by the river, who had not fulfilled Alarana's desire, had no further luck in their caribou hunting.

Told by Atangaushaq from Utokok River.

THE MONSTER MOUSE FROM COL-VILLE RIVER, AND THE TWO BROTHERS WHO SLEW IT

FAR up country at Kangianeq, near the source of Colville River, the stream widens into a big narrow lake. In the middle of the lake lies an island, and on the island there lived a monstrous animal that was called Ugjuknarpak (Monster Mouse) because it closely resembled a field mouse, but with so hard and tough a skin that neither arrows nor harpoons nor knives could pierce it. It had also a long, long tail, which it would twist round its prey when attacking.

On their way to Nerleq to trade with the folk from Point Barrow, the inland dwellers from Upper Colville were obliged to sail their boats through this lake, past the island where the monstrous creature lived. Then their terror was great, for if they made even the slightest noise in passing, Monster Mouse would immediately spring up, attack the boats, and overturn them with its long, twisting tail. Then it would kill all the folk with its sharp teeth and eat them. In this way the inland dwellers became fewer and fewer every summer, and yet there seemed no help for it. For when the river broke up, they had to go down to the coast to buy blubber and before the river froze again they had to return the same way to their inland home to hunt caribou.

Once, so they relate, there was a man who loved his daughter so dearly that he could not endure the thought that she might perish on the way. So when the boats, of which there was a large train, started off, he placed her in one which carried only few people, few dogs, and no small children that might suddenly begin to cry. Things fell out just as the father had imagined, for the girl's party slipped through safely. But his own boat and all those near it were attacked, and all the passengers perished, merely because a dog snarled a little as they rowed past the island. Immediately Monster Mouse pricked up his ears, raised his powerful head, and leaped at the boats. In vain did many of the men shoot their arrows at its thick hide; in vain were many spears hurled at it from the kayaks. Weapons were of no avail. The boats were thrown about and crushed to pieces, and men, women, and children perished miserably. The young girl, who loved her father just as dearly as he had loved her, awaited her family's arrival all summer. When at last winter came, she knew that Monster Mouse had killed her father and mother and all her brothers. Shortly after this she married, and when the time came, she gave birth to a child.

Her child was a boy, who soon became a big sturdy lad, strong and broad of figure. When he was old enough to understand, his mother would say to him again and again:

"Now you are a boy, and some day you'll be a man, but alas! never, never will you be strong enough to avenge your grandfather and your grandmother, and your mother's young brothers."

This she said to inflame his mind and to make him understand from the very first that it behooved him, and him alone, to avenge his mother's kinsfolk. He received the name of Woodpecker (Kugshavak) and before long he began to acquire skill in all kinds of sports. His powers grew in advance of his years, so that not only was he stronger than other boys of his age, but he also surpassed them in swiftness. Thus he grew up, tall, broad-shouldered, and swift, and every year his mother and father took him with them on the dangerous river journey. When they went past the island where Monster Mouse had his abode, his mother would point to it and impress upon him that the one great achievement in the world that awaited him was to kill this animal. But at the same time she would sigh and whisper that Woodpecker would never be strong enough to undertake this great revenge.

When he was still quite young his mother gave birth to another boy who was given the name of Comrade (Ilaganeq). He was born with strange hands, webbed between the fingers, which soon grew to resemble the flippers of the bearded seal. His mother told him, too, about the destruction of his kin. Like his brother, he grew up practising all kinds of sport, and always his mother filled his mind with bitter thoughts of revenge.

As soon as Woodpecker was big enough, he was given a kayak, and it was not long before he astonished everyone with his swiftness, his dexterity and his daring. But Comrade, who could not handle a kayak's paddle because of his deformed hands, became instead a great swimmer. While still a small boy he began to practise in the lakes, and within a short time he had learned to swim under water as long as the slender bearded seal.

Thus the two brothers grew up, both surpassing ordinary men in all kinds of skill. Their power and ability were uncommon, nay, they were champions whom one could scarcely believe to be born of an ordinary woman. Yet their mother told them again and again that they would never be strong enough to avenge their kinsmen. Daily they went to the river, where for hours one would row in his kayak, and the other would swim in the water like a seal. It is told that one day Woodpecker rowed up the river toward their dwelling, where there was such a strong current that no one had ever tried to row against it. Yet he did it easily, and even had two large caribou bulls in tow. Folk stood speechless beside the tents and stared at him, and when he cleared the foaming rapids they all burst out into shouts of applause. This seemed to make him increase his speed; the two caribou were whirled round and round, and he rowed so violently that they were seen now above the water, now below, just as if they were alive. And he rowed the kayak so powerfully in to the bank that it stood high and dry on land, with the two bulls lying beside it.

Now the mother thought the time was ripe for revenge, but first her sons would have to supply their parents with meat. The brothers went hunting and came home with caribou, many, many caribou, so that their meat gibbet was filled with flesh and hides. Not until there was room for no more did the two brothers set off to fight the monster, Woodpecker in his kayak, Comrade running along on the shore or swimming in the river. Thus they reached the notorious island and stole ashore, where soon they set eyes on their enemy. It was early morning, and the dew still gleamed on the grass. Monster Mouse had just awakened and was yawning sleepily. So huge were its jaws that they framed the whole horizon.

Before beginning the attack, the two brothers surveyed the land. There was a plain between the lake and the river, but the brothers were of the opinion that it was not too wide for them to run across, should flight be necessary. Now they approached the place where the Monster Mouse lay, Woodpecker in his kayak, Comrade swimming alongside. But scarcely had the animal set eyes on them than it rose up and ground its teeth, and rushed toward the kayak. Pretending to be frightened, Woodpecker turned around and rowed hurriedly toward the plain. At the same moment Comrade, who had been swimming under water, rose to the surface, and so swiftly did he swim that he cut the water like a frightened seal. Instantly Monster Mouse turned against him, but both brothers reached the plain safe and sound, and ran with all their might until they neared the river, where they stopped for the final battle. Monster Mouse thought himself sure of his prey, but the swift and nimble young men leaped aside every time his jaws opened over them. Leaping and dodging, they had time to take a closer look at the animal. Its hide was thick and invulnerable, but at one place of its neck they saw a slight wrinkle between its tight muscles. Perhaps it could be wounded there. Both brothers had flint knives with long wooden hafts. When their skillful dodging had driven the animal to the highest pitch of frenzy, Woodpecker sprang forward and drove his knife deep into the vulnerable spot in its neck. Instantly it turned against him, but at the same moment Comrade rushed ahead and stabbed it from the other side. The blood gushed out and it began to grow exhausted, and its movements became slower. Again and again the brothers assailed it, each time with greater ferocity, until finally it sank to the ground and died. Their old arch enemy was slain. Now the brothers examined it and found many arrow points and broken flint knives sticking in its hide. At last all the men who had in vain defended themselves with these weapons were avenged. But still more was to be done. The young men cut off the monster's head at the weak spot in the neck and carried it to a place by the river that is called Ivnaq. Here they set it up, so that all boats passing up and down the river should see that the dreaded enemy had been slain. This happened long ago. But the head, huge as a walrus head, is still to be seen. Its teeth have fallen out but there are traces of big tusks, and it can clearly be seen that the monster had a long gristly snout like that of a field mouse.

The head is now nearly withered away with age, yet people are still afraid of it. No one may speak loudly there, all row by whispering, and even the dogs are muzzled so that they cannot utter a sound.

The two brothers went home and told their mother about the feat they had accomplished. And for the first time in their lives they saw her smiling and happy. For at last her father and mother and brothers were avenged, and the avengers were her sons. This is the story of Woodpecker and his brother Comrade. They did a great many other deeds and won great fame in all lands. But we shall hear of that another time.

Told by Sagluaq from Upper Colville River.

THE TWINS WITH THE DOGS' EYES

MANY folk dwelt in a settlement by the sea. They had a chief, and the chief had a daughter who, as usual, did not want to marry. Many young men came and wooed her in vain; they were always sent away. At the same settlement there lived a man and his wife who were growing old without any children, and they were poor. At last, when they had almost given up all hope, the woman bore twins. But it was not a joyous event, for one of the children was quite blind, and the other had only one eye. The mother nursed them and looked after them as well as she could, but as they grew bigger, the folk refused to have two such monstrosities indoors, and so a little shelter was built for them out-of-doors beside the house. Here the mother had to go out to them and nurse them.

In all other respects the twins were a sturdy pair of lads; they were clever at going out and looking after themselves, and could eventually talk quite clearly. Sometimes the mother noticed that when all others slept they often began to laugh about something that amused them, and howled so much with laughter that she could not sleep. The brother with the single eye would let the blind one grope after something or other, and every time he missed it they laughed.

There was something else still more remarkable which the mother discovered later. They were in the habit of going out every morning, the one-eyed boy first, the blind one afterwards. But one day she noticed that the blind one went just as quickly as his brother, and now she saw, to her great surprise, that they had learned to take the sound eye out and to set it into the blind boy's eye socket, whereupon they cast a spell over it so that it became potent in place of the dead eye.

So the two brothers lived as good comrades, taking turns at using the only eye they had; but one night they were chattering about their misfortune when the single-eyed one suddenly hit upon the idea of taking an eye from a dog and setting it into his eye socket, and lo! he could actually see with it. So he took another eye from another dog and gave it to his blind brother, the whole thing taking place under magic songs, and now both of them had suddenly acquired full sight.

One day someone shouted that a stranger was coming. He was a wooer of the chief's daughter, a handsome and very fine man with a beaded band round his brow. All the people assembled in the feast hall, but here the two brothers had never been permitted to come.

While the feast was going on they peeked in at the window, and when they saw the handsome young wooer standing inside, the one-eyed one said:

"Brother, let's take his eye!" And the twins' speech had such power that the eye came through the window to them, so that now both of them had two eyes. But the unfortunate wooer became ill and burst into tears; he had to drive back to his home, paying those who helped him with his fine beaded band.

The twins grew up and got a kayak of the kind that has two manholes and they often went seal hunting with bladder harpoons. One day they rowed out in fine still weather and began to pursue a young seal far out at sea. Before they had harpooned it, they were overtaken by a mist so thick that they could scarcely see each other; it was utterly still, and they had no notion in what direction they were rowing. But they rowed and rowed and kept on rowing. At last it grew dark; and now they took turns in sleeping and rowing. Gradually the mist began to thin, and they saw something dark ahead. It was a mountain which rose steeply from the sea, and they followed the coast till they came to a headland. Here they tried to go ashore, but they had now sat so long in the kayak that they were quite numb. They were also hungry and had nothing to eat. After a short rest, during which they tried to revive their muscles, they rowed farther along the coast until they caught sight of smoke that came from a house, a solitary house with a meat gibbet.

Outside the house stood an old woman, and when she saw them, she cried out:

"Well, well, grandchildren! Have you come at last? That's a comfort! Come on in."

An old man sat inside the house, and he said:

"Dear children, it is good you came. It was I who called you."

Then they had to have something to eat. The old woman busied herself at the entrance to the house and presently came back and sat down. Shortly after, something rustled in the entry, and a piece of walrus skin came in of itself, a skin of the kind that is used as a tray for meat; it came gliding in, right up to the twins, opened of itself, and lo! there lay a little seal inside. A woman's knife rolled out and cut the seal up and put it into the cooking pot without anyone touching it, and when the seal was cut up, the walrus skin glided back again to the entry. It was a magic tray.

For some time the two brothers lived in the remarkable house, and the walrus skin used to come gliding in on the floor every time they were hungry. But at last they grew homesick and wanted to go away. The old man gave them dried caribou meat, a heavy load. They were to carry it and to leave the next day. The old people said: "Now, if at any time you should be in need, you must merely say: '*Nauk amigssaq?*' ('Where has the skin tray gone?') Then the walrus skin which you have seen here will come of itself, and it is a magic tray which will always bring you food."

Next day they took leave of the two old folk and went out into the house entry. But here a strange thing befell them: they walked on and on without ever coming out of the passage. It was as if this entrance to the house of the two old folk stretched over the whole world. At last they had eaten all their provisions and still they wandered on through the passage. So greatly did the old couple love the twins that they did not want them ever to get out of their house, and the house entry grew for every day's journey they made.

At last, however, they succeeded in coming out in the open air and now they remembered that the old folk had said to them when they took their leave:

"Turn round and look after us when you come out of the house."

And they turned round but saw nothing, no house, only land and ice. Remarkable indeed were the spirits they had visited.

They were near the land, hurriedly caught a seal, and now continued along the coast. In the evening they came to a dwelling where there were many men. They hid and waited for the people to go to rest. It was late evening before they dared enter the outermost house, where there dwelt an old man and his wife.

"Where do you come from?" they asked.

The brothers told where they came from, and the old folk said:

"There dwells a young chief here who murders all strangers. He will send you an invitation immediately, merely to get at you and kill you."

And sure enough! Food had scarcely been placed in front

of the twins than faces showed at the window; they were folk who had run up to tell the chief that guests had come to the settlement. A little later three men came in with tears in their eyes; they wept because they had been punished for laziness. Still more came in, and they all said that the two brothers must come up to the feast hall. The twins went up and met the chief in short trousers and short house *kamiks*. He was furious. Who should he be but the father of the young man whose eye they had stolen! And when he saw the twins he shouted as loud as he could:

"And you imagine that I shall let you live!"

The son still lay sick in the top bunk of the feast hall, and his father ordered his drum to be brought out forthwith, shouting:

"Do you really think you are going to live? Look at these men whom you see for the last time!"

And now the chief began to show his skill as a *shaman*. He rocked his head to and fro and crunched walrus tusks between his teeth. This was his way of showing his strength. But one of the twins stepped forward and cried:

"*Nauk amigssaq?*" And immediately a walrus skin came gliding in from the house entry over the floor, and without anyone being able to see who did it, first the son and afterwards the chief himself were laid on this skin tray, and in vain he shouted in mortal dread:

"Take my wives! I will do you no harm!"

But the woman's knife did its work without anyone being able to see who it was that flayed. First it cut off the son's head, and afterwards the chief's, and it flayed them just as if they had been seals. No one uttered a word. Terror had seized the folk of the settlement. Nobody wanted to defend the chief, for they hated him because he used to kill all the strangers who visited them; and he robbed men of their wives so that nobody could feel safe on account of his wickedness. But the two brothers avenged all those who had suffered wrong, and then went home to their country and to their parents.

Told by Apákag.

MISANA, WHO WAS SWEPT AWAY
TO THE LAND OF BEADS

THERE was once a young man who was called Misana. He was so young that he had just begun to get a small beard, yet he was a powerful hunter, who hunted walrus in all kinds of weather. But one day he, together with a comrade, was overtaken by a land gale with a snowstorm, and the waves broke over them so that they had to let themselves drift before the wind, away from land, out to the open sea. They grew weary and tried to bind their kayaks together to get some rest, but the waves were so high that they threatened to crush the kayaks, which could no longer maneuver quickly. So once more each had to struggle for his own life, and almost immediately afterwards the kayak of Misana's comrade overturned and came up no more.

Misana did not know whither he was drifting. He merely tried to hold himself up against the seas and to take good care that his paddle was not wrested from his grasp. Farther and farther out he drifted, till he came to a big ice floe; he let himself be washed up on it and got a little rest, but it was not long before the waves ate up the big ice floe, and again he had to go on in his kayak. How long he had drifted around he did not know, but when the storm cleared up a little he could just glimpse the high land of King Island like a little dot on the horizon. Now that he knew where he was he seemed to gain new strength, and he set his course for the mainland from which he had come. He rowed and rowed until he was near enough to discern the trees on the coast, but then came the same land storm again, sweeping over him thick with snow, and against his will he had to let himself be borne seaward by the waves. Now and then he could rest a little on the ice floes which he encountered. In one place, where he had approached a big ice field which for some time withstood the storms, he caught a little baby seal and got food just when his hunger was beginning to overwhelm him. He now understood that it was necessary to make his provisions hold out as long as possible, and he therefore satisfied himself with merely taking a mouthful at a time, when he could no longer restrain his hunger.

Many days passed thus under ceaseless storm, and when at last Misana could no longer sit up for weariness and seemed almost insane for lack of sleep, he bound four gut-skin covers round the manhole so that no water could pour in, and crawled down to the bottom of his big kayak, where he could lie outstretched while the waves tossed him about and swept him wherever they pleased. The storm continued.

This soon grew intolerable, and he thought it would be easier to die, yet he held out. He ate as little as possible and went on living in his kayak without rightly understanding why he did not give a little tug at the gut-skin cover and let the waves stream in to put an end to the whole thing.

Thus he tumbled around on the sea, days and nights being alike to him, until he discovered that no light ever shone into his kayak any more. Hitherto he had just been able to glimpse the daylight through the thin kayak skin. Now it was always dark. Where was he? Perhaps at the bottom of the sea. He did not understand it, and at last loosened the gut-skin cover; it did not matter to him that the waves might rush in. Evidently he was at the bottom of the sea, now that all around him had become dark. He made a tiny opening in the cover, just big enough for one eye. If water rushed in, he was at the bottom of the sea; if not, he must have been washed up on land in some place or another during the night. But it must be in a place with a long night.

He stared out with one eye, and as no water came in, he opened the manhole entirely. Clearly he was washed far up on land, but all about him was pitch darkness.

He felt a great relief. He tried to creep out of the kayak, but his legs were stiff and could not support him. His arms still felt strong, and for a long time he remained in his kayak, rubbing himself all over his body to put life into his muscles. This helped so much that he could creep out and crawl up on a bank and wait for daylight. But now that he could lie still on the ground and no longer was tossed about

in his kayak, he was overwhelmed by a great weariness. He
wrapped his storm covers closely about him and lay down
to sleep, so as to be thoroughly rested when at last the day
would come.

He slept long, awakened and slept again until at last he
was quite rested. But it was still pitch dark around him. He
rose and tried to accustom himself to the darkness, staring
into it to see if he could discern anything. All he could distinguish was a loud roaring noise in the air, sometimes near
sometimes far. Sadly he groped his way back to his kayak.
But when he reached the shore, he got his hands full of small,
smooth, round particles. He put one of them into his mouth
and discovered that there was a hole through it, and now
he took the string from his storm jacket and strung it with
the wonderful stones. They must be rare things, so he took
the string from another coat and did the same with that;
then he attached the two strings to his shoulders and fumbled onward to find out where he was. In vain he waited for
daylight. He grew drowsy and tired from the darkness, lay
down to sleep, awakened, slept again; and when at
last he was sure that he must have been there many days,
a thought occurred to him. He remembered having once
heard of Qasuilaoq, the land of eternal darkness, which lay
somewhere at the end of the world, and where there were
only nights and no days. And now he understood that the
noise in the air came from the motion of the earth; he was
standing at the end of the world, and the roaring came from
the mighty abyss that encompasses the earth.

Misana was standing at the end of the world.

Thus Misana was saved from the sea, but had come to a land that was no real land after all.

Again he sat thinking for a long time until he decided to continue the journey, if possible. He turned his kayak so as to have land to the right, for he believed that he must go in that direction to come back to the world of men where day and night alternated.

He rowed on and on in the darkness, without knowing how long. Suddenly he noticed something floating in the water. The sky had begun to lighten a little, and he rowed up to the object and discovered that it was a dead seal. At the same moment the joy of living came back to him, and he knew that he would do his very best to return to men once more. He followed the coast and whenever he was tired he went ashore to rest. His strength returned more and more. Every morning the strip of dawn on the horizon grew higher and higher; the light increased, and he approached the regions where day alternates with night.

At last it grew so light that he could see his surroundings, and now he discovered that his kayak, which had become strangely heavy to row, was completely overgrown with something that resembled hair. He was thirsty, and searched for fresh water. He found a little lake and started to drink when for the first time he saw his image in the water. He had to laugh aloud when he realized that his hair, beard, eyelashes, and eyebrows, nay, all the hair on his face, was gone. It had all been whizzed off at the end of the world. He examined the stones he had gathered, and only now did he discover that they were *sungaujarpait,* the famous and very costly big beads that were said to be found only at the end of the world. Too late did he regret that he had not taken many more with him. But he was happy to have been saved from the abyss, and made his daily journeyings longer so as to reach human dwellings sooner. He knew now where he was, and there came to his mind many tales which he had heard old folks relate of the land of eternal darkness. And it was clear to him that he must still experience dangerous adventures before he reached men.

One day it seemed as if the water about him congealed; it became heavy to row through, and he discovered that it was full of small gray fish. They swam about him in such teeming multitudes that he could scarcely get his kayak through. This was, then, the sea of the gray fish. It was from here that one came to men's settlements.

He rowed on and came to the sea of salmon. Here the water was in the same way filled with big powerful salmon, which he could push through only by the skin of his teeth. He had not rowed long in clear water before he met new difficulties. He came to a sea that was thronged with huge shoals of swordfish. He did not, however, become afraid of them, for he had heard that they must be like men, because they flayed their prey in just the same manner; so he rowed fearlessly in among the shoals and came safely through.

In the same fashion he came through the sea of the speckled seal. And to the sea of the whales, where whales swam in such vast schools that some of them lay almost high and dry; sometimes there would be one of them that would suddenly rise right out of the water, and all this filled the old whale hunter with such delight that he remained there many, many days, merely to look at them and rejoice over the beautiful huge animals.

At last he came to the sea of the walrus. These, too, lay in huge herds, some of them with their tusks shining in the sun; others merely showing their backs over the water's surface. Now he knew that he could not be far from men, and he hastened more than ever. One evening, when he was going to rest on shore, he found mounds cast up from the earth, and now he was quite certain that he would meet men. And, sure enough, the very next day he discovered big meat gibbets of driftwood and two houses not far from the shore.

It was long before anyone caught sight of him. At last he rowed nearer the houses, thinking it better to show no fear. It might even be that the others were afraid of him, taking him to be drowned and dead. At last two men came out; they stood and stared in terror at the stranger, who was entirely bald, without hair, or beard, eyelashes or eyebrows! They believed that he was a spirit, and wanted to flee. But Misana burst out laughing and shouted: "Just come nearer and have no fear; you'll find that I am an ordinary man and not at all dangerous!" This speech calmed the men, and they came down and helped him out of his kayak, for after his long row, his legs were still so stiff that he could not walk; the two strange men had to hold him by the arms to help him up to their house. For this welcome and reception Misana gave each of them a bead, and there was no end to their gratitude and joy over the costly gift.

At first the people at the settlement were afraid of Misana, but when it dawned upon them that he was in truth no ghost, they gave a song festival in his honor. He had then recovered so completely that he could beat the drum and take part in the dance. Misana's leaps caused great astonishment among his hosts. They were walrus in the shapes of men, and they were so heavy that they could only move at a walking pace and when they saw Misana dance, they shouted: "Aj! Aj! Aj! He lifts himself from the ground like a bird!"

The people called themselves "Aivilingmiut," the walrus folk. They were a heavy broad-shouldered race of powerful strength. They had hardly any neck and only a flat nose. They wore garments of walrus skin, long garments which reached down to their feet. With these garments on they looked very big, but as soon as they took them off, they resembled ordinary men.

Misana remained there some time and married one of the girls, who bore him a son. But as soon as the boy grew big enough to crawl on the floor, Misana took his leave and went on his way, giving the mother two beads as a farewell gift.

"If one remains with a woman until her children grow up, one never gets away from her again, and I must return to my own land," said Misana, and rowed away. But the woman was so glad of the fine farewell gift that she did not feel the slightest grief over his departure; because she knew that now men would vie with each other to marry her.

Misana traveled farther, and he almost always succeeded

in reaching a settlement about winter time; he would remain there and marry one of the women, but as soon as he had children, and the children began to crawl on the floor, he would take his leave hurriedly, giving his wife two beads as a farewell gift.

One time he came to a settlement where there lived a mighty man by the name of Stormcoat (Tuilipak). He was the chief of his settlement, had five wives, and was feared by all. The youngest and handsomest of his wives had four brothers at the settlement, and Misana married her. Stormcoat was beside himself with jealousy, and it was clear that he was going to kill Misana if the latter did not forestall him. But it was well known that Stormcoat was no ordinary man who could be killed in the usual way. He had never been badly wounded, though there had been many who had tried to murder him. Therefore Misana thought out a ruse. He buried himself in the sand with his brothers-in-law, and Stormcoat was asked to come to this place to meet his young wife. Then the five men fell on him. But they stabbed him in all possible parts of the body without making the least impression on him, until it occurred to Misana to stab him in his big toe. At the same moment he fell dead, and his secret was revealed: Stormcoat had his heart in his big toe.

Misana married the young wife and as usual remained with her until their child began to crawl. She was the one of all the women he had liked best, and therefore he gave her four beads as a farewell gift. And there was great rejoicing that all this wealth came to the settlement.

So Misana rowed away and came to the land of the

Chukchis. These nomad folk had just been on a trading journey to Misana's land and related that the folk there had buried his clothing and other possessions many years ago because they thought that he had drowned. At this Misana became very silent, for he now understood that there would not be any luck for him if he returned to his home. So he took land on Diomedes Island in Bering Strait. He was then an old man who went with a stick, a man who had lived a knock-about life from the time he was a mere lad. But it is said that during all his journeying he had learned so many lovely songs that men always flocked around him to hear him sing.

Told by Qalajaq from Point Hope.

133

THE FALSE WOMAN WHO BECAME
A NIGHT OWL

THERE was once a caribou hunter who went hunting by the sea. He walked and walked and continued walking until he came to the mouth of a big and foaming river. There he heard a voice—a lovely voice singing a song, and he listened and listened, until he could distinguish the words.

> *"Come, come,*
> *Lonely hunter*
> *In twilight's stillness.*
> *Come, come,*
> *Long have I*
> *Missed thee—missed thee,*
> *Now will I*
> *Kiss thee, kiss thee!*

134

Come! Come!
Near is my nest.
Come! Come!
Lonely hunter
Even now,
In twilight's stillness!"

The hunter was overwhelmed by an irresistible longing. With all his might he ran after the sound, along the bank of the river, ran like a man who had lost his senses, until he saw a lovely young woman sitting on a cliff on the opposite river bank and beckoning to him. But the river was big and broad and foaming, and the hunter stopped irresolute until the woman again took up her song:

"Come! Come!
Lonely hunter,
Even now,
In twilight's stillness."

Immediately he throws off all his clothes and springs out in the river. And he swims on and on in the cold stream, is caught by the current, battles, battles desperately, sometimes above, sometimes under the water, until, half dead with cold, numb and exhausted, he reaches the other bank and runs up to the woman, who still sits upon the cliffs beckoning and smiling. But at the very moment that he reaches her, she bursts into scornful laughter, changes into a night owl and flies away laughing. Half dead with cold, the hunter staggers down again to the river. His clothes lie on the other bank—he must again take to the cold water. And he swims on and on, battles against the current, and finally gets across. But when his foot touches the ground, he sinks down, prostrated. He loses consciousness and freezes to death.

Here his comrades found him. And none understood what had happened to the great and famous caribou hunter. For he lay there naked and frozen to death, and just beside him lay his warm clothing.

All thought that he had lost his reason. No one knew the nature of the quarry he had hunted.

Told by Apákag.

THE MAN WHO TAMED THE FIRST CARIBOU

THERE was once a young man who was out hunting caribou. But he had his own method of hunting; he merely followed the caribou without killing them. He tired them out, keeping constantly after them and reappearing every time they tried to slip away from him. At last the animals were so exhausted that they no longer went out of his way, and in this manner they accustomed themselves to his scent, to his clothing, and to his voice, and they were no longer afraid of him.

This young man liked to live in lonely places far from other dwellings. But one day he began to long for men and visited his neighbors. When he returned to his solitude he had a young woman with him whom he married. After that he lived his life as was his custom, always following the caribou until he had tired them out. Time no longer seemed long to him now that he had a companion. The caribou gathered in flocks, and sometimes fresh flocks would join the first; thus the herd grew bigger and bigger and the animals became more and more tame. At last he no longer needed to be always with them. He built a house where his wife could live, and thither he returned when his clothes were worn out and he wanted his wife to renew them.

In summer and autumn, winter and spring, the young man was always with his reindeer,* which kept on increasing. He was clever in his treatment of them, and as he never frightened them or chased them unnecessarily, the time came when he could move his tent to the herd and become a man who lived entirely on tame reindeer. In this way the first reindeer herdsman came into being.

The herdsman lived happily with his young wife, who after a time bore a son. The child grew up quickly, and in a short time was so big that he could help his father guard the herd. They took turns in keeping watch. When the father was with the herd, the son remained at home, and vice versa. There were many wolves in the country where they lived; it was the land of the Chukchis and the wolves bit many of the reindeer to death.

One day the father came and upbraided his son for sleeping too long: it was his fault that the reindeer were bitten to death. This scolding the son took very much to heart, and one evening when the father was out with the herd, he clad himself in his best clothes and asked his mother to give

---

*Caribou are used for wild reindeer as distinct from the domesticated reindeer in Siberia and most parts of Alaska.

him the food he liked best. Then they went to rest, mother and son, and the mother noticed nothing unusual in her son's talk. Yet the young man's mind had been affected; during the night he drove a knife into his heart and killed himself. He could not survive his father's wrath.

Next morning the mother saw blood under the *briks*, and when she lifted up the reindeer skin the son lay dead on his couch. So deeply did she grieve over this that she wanted the father to discover for himself what had happened. So she dried the blood from the floor and again covered her son with his sleeping-skin. Evening came before the father returned home, and when he did not see his son ready to relieve him he again became enraged, thinking that the boy was again sleeping too long. With angry words he tore the skin aside—and found his young son lying dead on the *briks*! Too late he rued his hastiness, and the woman aggravated his sorrow to no purpose, crying: "It's your own fault! You have killed him yourself with your upbraiding!"

From now on there was silence in the house of the herds-man. He guarded his flock without gladness, and the woman thought only of the boy who had taken his own life. In the autumn the herdsman traveled afield and visited neighboring folk. Here he invited young men to come with him; they were to help him to kill long-horned bulls. This they did, and now he had the young men build two big tombs of reindeer horn, raised high above the ground, so that beasts of prey could not approach them. The dead son was laid on one tomb, and the father climbed to the other; from here he spoke thus to the young men who stood around him:

"Let this land of the tame reindeer be your land; let the animals live, never slay more than you need for food and clothing. Never sell them, but let them constantly multiply and increase. Live together with them and let them give you what you need, so that you can live a life without sorrows and anxieties."

This was the herdsman's speech. Then he divided his big flock among all the young men who had helped him, and when this was done he drove a knife into his heart just as the son had done. And he remained lying dead upon the tomb he had himself helped to erect. Thus died, so it is said, the first man who tamed reindeer; from him originate all the reindeer herds. And the two mighty arches of bulls' horn which were used as tombs for father and son are still displayed as a memorial of the first men who lived off tame reindeer.

Told by Atarnaq from Cape Prince of Wales.

THE STORY OF WOLF

THERE were once a man and his wife who lived without any neighbors by a great river. They had an only son to whom they gave the name Wolf. He was to have strong amulets to protect him if he should be in danger of his life, and so they gave him smoke from a fire, an ermine, and the guiding feather of an arrow.

The boy grew up and soon became a young man who could go caribou hunting with his father. One day he came to his father and said:

"Father, are there no other men at all in the world?"

"Yes, far, far away," answered the father.

"I'll go and search for them," said the son, and he made himself ready for the journey and set off. At his departure the mother gave him a bracelet of copper and three beads, saying: "All these you will need some day." And so he set out into the world to seek for men.

Wolf followed the river and after some days came to a big bend in the stream, a turning that led over high mountains. He walked on and on, but he never seemed to come nearer the mountain. Suddenly a woman showed herself before him, an old, old woman who stretched her arms up into the air and cried:

"I wonder whether you are the one who is to bring me gifts? If you are the one I'm waiting for, you shall have my grandchild."

Wolf gave her his copper bracelet and slept in her house that night. At his departure the old woman said:

"If you are ever in danger, just think of me and wish for my help, and you shall have it."

Wolf continued his way and came to a new bend in the river, a big turning that led him up over a ridge of hills. Again the same thing happened: he could make no progress. Suddenly an old man stood before him, stretching his arms in the air and saying: "Have you anything to give me? If you are the one I am waiting for, you shall have my grandchild. She will come running to meet you when you approach her dwelling. She is a skillful runner, but if you are more skillful than she, she shall be yours, for only he who reaches her house first, shall wed her."

The old man received a bead, and Wolf spent the night with him. The next day he set out, and the old man said to him:

"If you are ever in danger, just think of me and wish for my help and you shall have it."

The old woman and the old man were ghosts, they were

man and wife who were buried in two different places, and it was in their graves the young man had dwelt. When dead folk are afoot on earth their graves become houses. Now Wolf had won the ghosts' friendship and obtained their power and protection, and later that was to be of great gain to him.

Wolf walked and walked until he caught sight of a large settlement. He had scarcely set eyes on it than a young and lovely girl came running to meet him. At once they began to run races with each other. She was a good runner, yet Wolf was swifter. He outran her and came first into her house. Here he was entertained with delicious food, and all were friendly and kind to him.

After the meal the young woman wanted to play ball with him. A ball was hung under the roof from a short cord, and they were to spring with both legs together and try to hit the ball. He lost, and she won.

Now the young woman wanted to play "Drying-rack," a jumping game which is so called because the thing one jumps over resembles the drying-rack above the blubber lamps where the women dry footgear and clothing. A number of rungs are fastened to two beams like steps in a ladder, and the beams are placed horizontally a good distance from the ground; then one hops with both legs together over the rungs, first over one, then over the second, and so on. In this game again he lost, and she won. Then they became man and wife.

They lived happily together throughout the winter. Then

came the spring, and caribou hunting began. Wolf wanted
to set off, but he must have his wife with him.

"No, that you can't. All the women who go caribou hunting disappear, they vanish," said his brothers-in-law. "You
can't take your wife with you."

Yet Wolf was bound to have his wife with him to help
him dry meat; so his brothers-in-law said: "Do as you like,
stiff-neck!"

The hunters roamed inland; Wolf accompanied them and
never lost sight of his wife who walked beside him all the
time. The summer passed, and nothing happened; the man
and woman were always together. When the first snow
began to fall they heaped some of their dried meat up in
caches and loaded the rest on sledges with which they aban-
doned the hunting camp and started back to their home.

One day Wolf saw a bull and began to hunt it, his wife
running in front of him. He shot off his arrow, but while
aiming he had for an instant taken his eyes off his wife—and
now she was gone! Lost without trace, without the tiniest
footprint.

Wolf sat down and wept, and the brothers-in-law, who
were also on the road home, came up to him and said: "Now,
what did we say! No woman can go hunting. Now it is too
late for you to cry, you stiff-neck. Come along home with the
rest of us: there is nothing else to be done."

"No," said Wolf, "I will die in the place where I have last
seen my wife." And again he burst out crying and could not
stop. He would not eat, and he would not hunt. He would not
move from the spot. He wanted to die.

But one day a sound reached his ears. The noise grew and came nearer and nearer. He looked up and discovered two strange young men, one in trousers of wolverine skin, the other in trousers of wolfskin. They were a wolverine and a wolf in human shape. And they came up to him and said: "We know where your wife is."

"Lead me there immediately," shouted Wolf.

"No, that we can't do. It is far, far away. She is hidden in a valley near a high mountain where traveling is very dangerous. But if you will give us a bead we will tell you all we know."

The two strange men each received a bead and told Wolf what they knew about the way. He sprang up immediately from where he had lain, and ran and ran with all his might in the direction which they had indicated.

After running for five days he came in sight of a high mountain. Near the mountain there was a valley, and there, far, far away, lay also a house with a big meat gibbet outside, and when he came nearer he saw caribou whole and unflayed, hanging by their horns on the gibbet. Carefully he stole nearer, and at some distance from the house caught sight of a crane, and close by the shelter wall of the entrance, a lynx. On the game gibbet lay an eagle's skin. The crane and the lynx were sentinels, and it was an eagle who lived there, an eagle in human form. Its skin lay on the gibbet when it was not a bird.

Wolf drew out one of his amulets and changed himself into an ermine, crept in under the snow, and came past the crane without its discovering him. Then he went on, still in

Wolf changed himself into an ermine and hid in the shelter wall
in front of the house entry.

the shape of an ermine. But when he was going past the game gibbet, the eagle's skin opened its eyes; eagles are wakeful folk: even the empty skin kept watch. The ermine slipped under the snow and safely past the lynx, who noticed nothing. Then he hid in the shelter wall in front of the house entry.

Wolf kept himself well hidden and saw no one until late in the evening. Then the eagle came out with Wolf's wife. and when Wolf saw her his heart beat so strongly that he could scarcely keep himself quiet. After that the whole place within the shelter wall became filled with women, stolen women. After a while they went back to the house, and silence reigned. But Wolf followed them, invisible as his smoke amulet, and smoked into the eyes of the eagle, so that the latter at last became drowsy and fell into a deep sleep. Immediately Wolf awakened all the women and whispered to them that now they might flee, if they desired to go home. All their clothing was hidden high under the roof, and he had to take it down for them before they could get away. But before he himself took his departure he wanted to render the eagle harmless, and, finding a big flint ax, he hacked its head off. At the same moment there came a big noise, and the door near which he stood vanished. He found himself within a pitch-dark smooth rock cavern and had to grope around to find the way. But high up under the roof there came a little streak of light from a crevice in the cliff, and taking on the form of his third amulet, the steering feather of an arrow, he shot out through the crevice.

The crane and the lynx had become powerless through

the eagle's death, and all that now threatened him and the women were the hindrances which the soul of the slain eagle would conjure forth over the way they must go. He looked out over the land: women were running everywhere, in all directions; they were hurrying home to their dwellings, where their husbands had probably given up all hope of seeing them again.

Wolf set off after his wife, and as he knew that the slain eagle would pursue no one but him with its magic, he looked around carefully while running beside her.

"You love contests," he said to her. "Show me now how swift you can be!"

At this moment he heard a roaring noise behind him as if of stones striking the ground, and when he looked round he descried a mighty stone which came rolling after them, plowing up all the ground around it. The stone, which came rolling over the plain with the speed of an avalanche, was sent out by the slain eagle's soul, and no living man could avoid it. But Wolf thought of the old ghost who had promised to help him, and he called on him. Instantly they were standing beside his grave, which became a house, and the ghost came out and dragged them into the house while the stone turned aside and rolled past.

Wolf remained with the old ghost until they could neither hear nor see the stone. Then he and his wife set off and continued the race to their dwelling. But scarcely had they come out on a big open plain where no cover was to be found than the stone again came in sight with a cloud of earth and pebbles about it. This time Wolf invoked the old ghost woman to whom he had given his mother's copper bracelet. Like her husband, she came at the very moment he called her, and she gave them shelter in her grave and sent the stone on past her house.

"It is best that you should remain here till morning," said the ghost woman, "for the eagle's weapon must have time to exhaust its strength."

Wolf and his wife remained in the grave overnight and set out again the next day. As usual, they ran with all their might and got well on towards their dwelling. In the middle of the day, while crossing a plain, they saw again the eagle's rolling stone, but it had lost most of its magic power and had become quite small and was rolling slowly and harmlessly over the ground.

At the settlement there was great rejoicing over Wolf's exploit, and even from strange, distant settlements men came traveling to thank him. They were men who had at one time lost their wives and who had now got them back after the robber of women had been slain. All the grateful husbands made Wolf their chief, and he lived happily to the end of his days, loved and respected by all.

This is the story of how Wolf lost his wife and afterwards got her back again.

Told by Apákag.

A GIRL'S AFFECTION, WHICH FIRST KILLED A MAN AND AFTERWARDS BROUGHT HIM BACK TO LIFE

IT IS told that everyone admired Imogê. He was a chief's son and a great hunter, always on the move. There was only one thing wrong with him: he wouldn't marry.

At the same settlement there lived an old woman and her grandchild, a little girl. Every evening all the young men and women assembled to play ball, and the little girl used to go to watch the ball players.

Time passed, and it was not long before she was a young girl who could take part in the games herself. And so it happened that she fell in love with Imogê.

One evening she came home from the ball game weeping. Her grandmother patted her on the cheek and said:

"What's the matter? Who has been unkind to you?"

"Imogê has. He pushed me!"

"Never mind that," said the old grandmother.

But the same thing happened again. The young girl often came home from the ball game, weeping, and she always said that it was Imogê who had been unkind to her.

But one evening she came home weeping worse than ever, and her clothes were torn into rags.

"Who did that?" asked the grandmother.

"Imogê did it," answered the girl. The old grandmother never suspected that she lied; for she did not know that the girl had fallen in love, and that it was from sheer despair over Imogê's indifference that she told all these lies. So the grandmother was angry and wanted to avenge her grandchild. She was versed in witchcraft, and it was an easy matter for her to compose a magic formula which caused sickness. One evening, when the girl came home again, weeping and complaining about Imogê, the old grandmother said:

"To-night, when folk are lying down to sleep, you must hide in a corner of the wind screen by Imogê's father's house. You must stand right under the snow wall, so that no one can see you. Imogê is in the habit of going out every evening before going to sleep. As soon as he has been out and goes in to lie down, you must take a bit of snow from the place where he has stood and bring it to me."

When the time came, the girl did as her grandmother had said. One by one the men and the women came out, last of all Imogê, and when he went in, she cut a bit of snow out of the place where he had stood and brought it to her grandmother.

The grandmother immediately recited magic words over the lump of snow and put it into a little bag made of the fine thin membrane round a caribou's heart. This bag she hung over the fire, so that the snow melted, whereupon she bent over the bag, and said over and over:

"May Imogê have pains."

The next day Imogê became ill. He felt pains, and so great were they that nobody could help him. The same evening he died.

All grieved for the fine young man who had died so suddenly, the great hunter who was so much thought of by all. On the very same day Imogê's corpse was laid in the feast hall and everybody left the settlement. Nobody would remain where Imogê was dead, nobody dared go hunting from the place where Imogê lay as a corpse. The only ones who remained behind were those to whom no one paid any attention: the old woman and her grandchild.

It was midwinter, and the two women now lived quite alone together, without any man to hunt for them. And it was not long before they began to feel the pinch of want.

But the young girl could not forget Imogê. She went on thinking about him. And one night when she could not sleep, she rose and went into the feast hall where he lay as a corpse. But first she gathered fuel and laid it outside. Then she groped her way into the dark feast hall, feeling before her with her hands to find the way in the darkness.

They had hung Imogê under the roof to protect him from the beasts of prey. The frozen corpse was swathed in caribou skin. The young girl groped forward, and when she had come to the corpse, she cut it down. Then she fetched the kindling she had gathered, and lit a fire in the fireplace.

"Deep affection's strongest thinking
Lifts the dead man's frozen body
Up to earth's own warmest life."

The fire quickly began to flare up and give warmth, and while she lifted the corpse on her back, she began to go round the fire with the frozen man in her arms. And before long Imogê began to thaw. Then the girl sang a song:

> *"Ja—ijai—ja*
> *Ja—ijai—ja—*
> *Deep affection's strongest thinking*
> *Lifts the dead man's frozen body*
> *Up to earth's own warmest life.*
> *Ja—ijai—ja—*
> *Ja—ijai—ja—*
> *Let again his spirit blossom,*
> *Let him once more dauntless travel*
> *Midst the other living creatures.*
> *Ja—ijai—ja*
> *Ja—ijai—ja."*

This song she went on singing, and now and again in between she cried with a loud voice:

"Imogê! Imogê! Imogê!"

Soon the body was no longer stiff. Still more ardently the girl cried:

"Imogê! Imogê!"

Slowly the life returned, and she heard him whisper quite softly:

"Yes, yes, what is it?"

Then the girl cried with all her might:

"You must wake up! You must wake up, Imogê! All your neighbors have left you."

And the girl continued going round the warm fire, shouting and calling him, until Imogê had come back to life. No one could tell from his appearance that he had ever been dead. Now they went gladly down to the old grandmother, and became man and wife.

Thus it came to pass that Imogê, who would not marry, got a wife, and they lived happily together to the end of their days. Now their bones are bleaching, and this story is finished.

Told by Apákag.

THE SPIRIT OF THE AIR HELPS A POOR BOY

BY THE coast of the great ocean there was a settlement with many inhabitants. Here lived a poor man and his wife. Often the natives of the place traveled over to the Chukchis, who owned tame reindeer, to exchange fine reindeer skin for lines of sealskin, but the poor couple could never go along, for they had nothing to trade with.

Then it happened that the woman bore a son, a miserable boy whose legs were so misshapen that his heels were in front of his toes. They called him Quarsaitko (Fright), and nobody believed that he would ever amount to anything.

One time the boy's father decided to accompany his neighbors to the land of the Chukchis; but he had nothing to trade with, and the chief scorned him for his poverty, saying:

"Strange man that comes such a long distance without

having anything to trade with, I will make you an offer: you shall have a gift if you can swallow the knee cap of a reindeer. Then I will give you a calfskin, and that you may well call a good exchange."

The poor man knew well that it was impossible for him to swallow the knee cap of a reindeer, but he dared not refuse to try. So he tried it but became sick and vomited and returned home ashamed, scorned by all the strangers, who amused themselves over their chief's joke. As soon as the poor man came home, he seized his boy and told him what he had endured, and beat him thoroughly, crying:

"And I have to tell that to one who will never at any time be able to avenge me, to a wretched, misshapen boy."

The father did not do this from malice, but because he wanted to arouse the boy's mind. And after that it became a custom with him; often he laid hold of the boy and ill-treated him, saying the same words to him:

"And this I do to you, who will never at any time be able to avenge me."

Thus he reared his son to hatred and mistrust of others, and the boy was never happy, but felt hostile to all mankind.

One moonlight night when the boy was outside playing, he suddenly heard a sound in the air. The sound came nearer and nearer, and now a little boy became visible, a little boy who came floating down toward the ground with a big napkin of reindeer skin fluttering round him. It was the spirit of the air. First he hovered round and round the houses, then came to rest and began to talk, speaking thus:

A little boy came floating down toward the ground with a big
reindeer skin fluttering round him

"I come because I have pity for you. You suffer evil every day because they have scorned your poor father; but if you will make a blood offering to me, I will help you. While other men sleep, you must run around and practise all kinds of sports, and I shall make you strong and swift."

Thus spoke the babe who was no other than the spirit of the air, and then he vanished.

The misshapen boy was called Fright. From now on he never slept at night, for when others did not see him, he exercised his strength; and his feet took on their right shape. Soon he became a young man, big and strong as a giant; but nobody knew what great strength he had, for he always kept to himself.

The spirit of the air had given him a staff that was to be his only weapon against his enemies; and this staff he was to use the first time that sledges arrived from the settlement of the wicked chief of the Chukchis.

At last one day the sledges came, and now everyone believed that Fright was out of his mind, for he ran alone towards all the strange men, swinging his stick over his head, and shouted so that everyone could hear it:

"And so it was I who would never avenge my father whom you forced to swallow a knee cap!"

First the folk laughed at him, but it wasn't long before the whole settlement was seized with terror, for one by one he put to death all the Chukchis. And for every man that fell, he shouted his battle cry of vengeance. At last there were no more. Thus Fright fulfilled his father's expectations, and for every man he had slain he sacrificed blood to the spirit of the air.

This was Fright's first battle. Afterward he became a much feared man-slayer in all lands, and put to death all the men he came near. And every time he slew men he sacrificed blood to the spirit of the air, crying:

"And so it was I that would never avenge my father!"

Fright lived always far from men, and his abode was the top of a mountain with a view to all sides; for all lands had now joined forces to put him to death. One day, as he lay in a mountain cavern, stones came rolling down, one after another, and Fright sprang up and ran up on the mountain to see who it was that threw them. He saw a man and cried to him:

"Why do you do that?"

"Because I want to try to put Fright to death."

"I am Fright, and no other!"

"What! Then come home with me!" Fright did so, and he killed this man also and all his family, in the same way that he had slain all the others.

But that was his last act of manslaughter, for suddenly he heard a voice up in the air, crying, "He-he!"

It was the spirit of the air that came fluttering down in circles; it was quite bloody about its mouth with all the blood offerings, and it cried:

"Stop! Stop! I can't drink any more blood. If you slay more men I must eat you."

With this word the spirit of the air soared upward and vanished.

Fright turned back to his dwelling and slew no more men. He married the daughter of the chief, and afterwards hunted caribou with the staff he had used to slay men. And he became a mighty hunter and a big man among his neighbors.

Told by Apákag.

THE SKULL THAT SAVED THE GIRL

THERE were once a man and his wife who lived by the great river Kobuk, up-country between Kotzebue and Koyukuk. They had one daughter and three sons but knew no one else. The young men were skillful hunters who often sailed on the river in their skin boats; and so much game had they slain of caribou and wolf, wolverine and fox, that they had built four large meat gibbets of split tree trunks to hold the meat. Their house stood near the river, but so thickly stood the trees of the wood that they had had to clear a path to the river. Although they were all so skillful, they never went down to visit the people by the sea.

One day the young daughter was down at the river to fetch water; she was standing and gazing over the stream, up and down, when to her great astonishment she caught sight of the first strange kayak she had ever seen. A stranger came rowing up the river, and as soon as she was certain that she had made no mistake she ran home and told about it. With all the others she returned to the river, and here they stood on the bank as the kayak put in.

"Ah, here we live and know nothing at all about other men," said the young girl's father in welcome. "Do come up to our house." The stranger came ashore, and when they asked him where he had come from, he said that he was from the seashore.

"What do you want up here?"

"I have no wife, and now I am out to find one for myself."

"That won't be difficult for you," said the young girl's father, "for here we have a young daughter who has no sweetheart."

The young man accepted the invitation and immediately married the girl, whose name was Neruvana. He settled down by the river and from now on hunted in company with his brothers-in-law. The winter passed, and the spring broke up the river ice. The time for hunting had come. "Where do you hunt caribou?" asked the brother-in-law one day. "Everywhere," answered the others, "but we like best to go upstream in our boats."

"Neruvana and I will also go reindeer hunting," answered the brother-in-law, "but we would rather travel alone; then it won't be so long before we come home again."

So they made ready and rowed away; when they came back again some days later, their boat was loaded with caribou.

In this way the man and wife often went out together.

And it might happen that the man left their camping ground alone and remained away many nights without the wife knowing where he was. Once when he had thus been out alone and came back, he said to her that they had better go down to see her family. They rowed down to the house, but no one came out to receive her. Neruvana went ashore and found them all, her father, mother, and brothers, lying dead—killed, murdered, stabbed to death! Beside herself with grief, she rushed down to her husband to tell him what she had discovered, but saw to her astonishment that he had already pushed off from land and sailed down the river. She shouted after him, and he answered that he would land immediately, yet he sailed on. She ran after him along the bank, without understanding, almost out of her mind, but when night fell he lay down on the opposite side of the stream, and she could not cross over to him. In this way he went on traveling, and Neruvana, who had nothing to eat, languished and became thin. At last she could run no longer. She had to walk very slowly, till the day came when she crept along the bank, feeling as if death were near at this time. She came to a little tributary, and as she had not the strength to cross it, she thought to herself: "I will die here, but first I will look about for a pretty place."

She found a place where there was high, soft grass; the sun shone, and there was shelter; here she lay down to die.

While she was lying here, she suddenly heard a sound and looked around but could see nothing. Every time she lay down she heard the same sound, a voice calling, but she could not distinguish the words; so she slipped off her hood,

"Little grandchild, you shall not die!" said the skull.

and now she heard the voice quite clearly. It said: "Grandchild, dear little grandchild, dig me out, dig me out!" Only now did she discover that she had lain down beside an old grave: her own grandmother's grave. She dug ardently, and at last found a bone, and now she heard close beside her:

"Little grandchild, you are on the right track. Take me out of the earth, help me out of the earth!" And a little later a skull lay before her; it spoke thus:

"Ah! little grandchild, you have really dug me out of the ground. Now you shall not die. First make yourself a shelter of twigs. After that you shall build yourself a little house of tree trunks and earth."

Neruvana did as her grandmother said, and while she worked at the shelter she laid the skull carefully on the ground, swathing it in soft grass.

"Make a fire, little granddaughter, we're freezing. Fetch dry brushwood and make a fire."

And Neruvana fetched brushwood, but did not know how she was to make a fire.

"Is there still a little flesh in my eye sockets, grandchild?"

"Yes, a little bit."

"Then pick it out with your forefinger and lay it on the brushwood. Shut your eyes and blow on it."

Neruvana did this, and immediately a strong flame flared up with delicious warmth, a fire that never went out.

They took a long rest before the fire, and the next day Neruvana built a little house. When she was ready, the grandmother said: "Go over to my grave and see if you can find a walrus tooth which was once my belt buckle."

Neruvana, who was still much exhausted by hunger, crawled over to the grave and found the buckle, and when she came back with it the grandmother said: "Set a tree trunk up at the side of our house and hang the walrus tooth behind it."

Neruvana did this, and then laid herself down again to sleep. But in the middle of the night the old grandmother cried: "Go out and take a peep at my belt buckle." And lo! when Neruvana came out, there lay a heap of dead hares outside the house, all with their heads crushed. They had run against the belt buckle and had killed themselves. This was the old grandmother's work; for as a ghost she was full of magic power.

Now, Neruvana prepared a fine meal, but the skull took no share in it. It only talked. They made bedclothes and garments of the hare skins. And it was not long before Neruvana again got flesh on her body and strength so that she could walk.

One day the grandmother said again that the walrus buckle should be hung outside the house. Night came and they heard many sounds outside, and when Neruvana went out, she found caribou after caribou lying dead by the house. They had died in the same way as the hares. Now they had a superabundance of meat, and Neruvana, who had now quite regained her strength, built their house bigger and better. Winter came, snow covered the ground, and the old grandmother began to hunt even the winter game with her walrus buckle. She caught wolf and wolverine and fox, and they dried the skins by the fire which never died. Thus they had all they needed; they had caught many caribou during the season when the calves had their fine, thin coat of hair. And Neruvana built a meat gibbet and filled it with winter provisions and skin.

One day the old grandmother said:

"This you must know, that the same fate has overtaken you which was once mine; therefore I had pity on you. Also, I would gladly avenge myself, and so I wished to return to the surface of the earth. We two have been married to the same sort of men, wicked men; it has been the misfortune of our lives. It was your own husband and no other who slew your father, your mother, and your brothers and sisters. My husband did the same thing with my relatives. But now we shall both have our revenge. Your husband, who believes you are dead of hunger, will one day come up the river again; it will be at the time the hunting begins, in spring. Now we have nothing to do but to wait and hold ourselves in readiness. You shall sew fine clothes of calfskin and trim them with bands of wolverine and wolf. I, too, shall have a pelisse which is as fine as yours. And when the river breaks up, you must build us a hiding place on the bank. Here we shall hide and wait for the umiaks; it will not be difficult for you to recognize your husband. You will see him lying in the middle of the boat like a big chief, puffed up and pompous and ready for new misdeeds. But I must be lying right beside your hiding place so that you can easily kick me into the river, and I shall give him a warm welcome!"

The winter passed, and the sun's warmth melted the snow, and the river ice burst with the current and the heat; the land became living, everything grew green, and summer came.

One day the old grandmother said:

"To-day the umiak comes which brings your husband up the river." This she could say because she was a ghost and knew everything that would happen. So they both hid on the river bank, and it wasn't long before many boats came round a headland a short distance below them. The boats, which were manned by folk they did not know, were allowed to pass; after that came the man they awaited, and he sat like a big man in the middle of his boat, self-important and quite unconscious of what awaited him.

Then his wife rose and cried:

"Boats! Boats!"

And her husband looked towards the bank and answered:

"Well, I never, my wife's alive!"

With these words he set his course towards land. At that moment the old grandmother said: "Now, now is the time!" And so Neruvana kicked the skull, and it flew over the water and fell down just beside the boat. Immediately the water began to boil in whirlpools, huge bubbling maelstroms that carried the umiak with them. All the folk on board perished, but the head came rolling back to the bank as if nothing had happened, and laid itself beside its grandchild. Not even the fine coat collar had become wet. The skull spoke and said:

"Now we have wrought the vengeance we desired, and can remain here till you grow old. Not until you die will I again leave the earth's surface. We shall live together, as we shall one day die together."

These were the words of the old grandmother. And herewith ends the story of the death's head which saved Neruvana from starving to death.

Told by Apákag.

THE WHALE'S SOUL AND ITS BURNING HEART

THERE was once a stupid and self-important raven who flew far, far out to sea. It flew and flew, farther and farther, and when it grew tired it began to search for land, but there was no land. At last it was so tired that it could barely hold itself hovering over the surface of the waters, and when all at once a great whale came up in front of it, it was so confused that it flew straight into its mouth.

For a moment all was darkness around it, a whistling and rippling, and just when it believed it must die, it tumbled straight into a house, a beautiful and dainty house where there were light and warmth. On the bunk sat a young woman who busied herself with a burning lamp. She rose and welcomed the raven kindly, saying: "You are welcome to be my guest if you will promise me one thing: you must never touch my lamp."

The raven, who was glad to have saved its life, hastened to reassure her that it would never meddle with the lamp, and then sat down on the bunk and began to notice how fine and clean it was in the little house. It was a whalebone house, built like the dwellings of men, and everything within was arranged after the fashion of men. But there was a remarkable restlessness about the young woman. She never sat still for any length of time; at short intervals she rose from the bunk and slipped out of the door. Only a moment passed, and she was in again; but immediately after, she was gone once more.

"What is it that makes you so restless?" asked the raven.

"Life," answered the young girl, "life and my breathing."

But this answer he did not understand in the least.

The raven, who had now become quieter and had forgotten his fear, began to grow curious.

"Why am I never to touch the lamp?" it thought; and every time the girl slipped out and it remained alone it felt a strong desire to break its promise and go over and finger the lamp just a tiny bit. At last it could no longer bridle its curiosity, and when the girl again slipped out at the door, it sprang over and touched the wick of the lamp. At the same moment the girl tumbled head foremost through the door, fell down on the floor and remained lying there, while the lamp went out.

Too late the raven rued what it had done. It staggered about in darkness, and the pretty bright house was no more. It was almost suffocated. It rambled about amid fat and blood, and it grew so hot in there that its feathers.fell off.

Half choked it tumbled around in the whale's belly, and only now did it understand what had happened.

The young girl was the soul of the she-whale, and she slipped through the door, out into the open air, every time the whale had to draw breath. Her heart was a lamp with a great and steady flame. Out of sheer curiosity the raven had touched the young girl's heart, and this had caused her death. The raven did not know that the fine and the beautiful is also fragile and easily destroyed, for it was itself stupid and hard to kill; and now it fought for life in blood and darkness. All that had formerly been fair and clean had now become foul and fetid.

At last it succeeded in slipping out the same way it had come in, and there it sat, a half-naked raven, greasy and dirty, on the back of a dead whale.

Here it remained, living off the carrion, tossed by wind and waves. Its wings were disabled with heat and blood, so that it could fly no more.

At last a storm drove it towards land, and the people saw the whale's carcass and rowed out in their umiaks to obtain the flesh and fat. When the raven saw them it changed itself into an ugly little swarthy and rumpled man, standing upon the whale.

He did not mention at all that out of sheer curiosity he had meddled with a heart and ruined something fair and beautiful. He only crowed exultantly: "It is I who have slain the whale! It is I who have slain the whale!"

And he became a big man among men.

Told by Pamik from Utokok River.

WANDER-HAWK, WHO WENT OUT INTO THE
WORLD TO UPROOT THE WICKEDNESS OF
LIFE AND THE TREACHERY OF MAN

WANDER-HAWK

A YOUNG man came out from the forests. No one knew from where. But he was born right in the heart of the country, and one winter day he came walking on snowshoes down to the coast at Silivik, east of the big Kobuk River. He was a youth, not yet of marriageable age, and he mixed fearlessly with the inhabitants of the coast in their settlement, going from house to house. The folk of Silivik called him the Woodman. He remained here till he was full grown. Then he took a wife and again went his way. He chose land on a headland of Silivik, alone with his wife, and they built their house in a spot which is still called the Shorecliffs.

The Woodman soon became a great hunter and trapper, and his house knew no want. Near the dwelling there was a river where he fished for salmon. Caribou he hunted far inland with bow and arrow; also white whales and young bearded seals in the sea from his kayak. Time passed, and they lived in prosperity and abundance. His wife bore him a son. Then a second, and a third, and a fourth son. Thus they had four sturdy boys; but after this they had no more children.

They lived always in their home by themselves and knew nothing of other company, never saw other people. Soon the eldest son was big enough to begin to hunt; he got a little bow and accompanied his father when he went after caribou. So the boy learned to hunt on land. When he grew a little older he got a kayak and rowed out to sea with his father. Here he learned to hunt white whale and young bearded seals. He also hunted dangerous land bears, and when he had destroyed many of them without his father's help, he got leave to look after himself. The young man became a great hunter, as his father was, and the father rejoiced over this and no longer forced himself to hunt as diligently as before.

Thus the Woodman and his family lived in happiness and abundance until misfortune befell them. One day the eldest son did not return from the chase. They waited in vain; they sought to no purpose: the young hunter was lost without a trace.

Father and mother mourned deeply and long, until at last they grew reconciled to their loss. There was nothing else to be done.

Then the second son became full grown and began to hunt with his father, and when he too, like his big brother, had felled many dangerous land bears without help, his father left him to his own devices—to hunt as he would.

But exactly the same thing happened to him as to his brother. One day he disappeared and returned no more. And so it came to pass with the third son and the fourth son: they all disappeared while hunting, and the parents became childless in their old age. They had no children to help them; they lived alone and knew nothing of other men. And both grieved deeply over their evil lot, now that they were old and could not expect to have more children.

Ancient folk have described their dwelling place, which was situated by a cliff between the hills of Quingmeq and the plain, by a place called Saunertoq. Here they lived, men say; here it was that they sought in vain for their vanished children, and here it was that they grew old without any likelihood of having more children.

THE WOODMAN AND HIS MAGIC CHILD

LONG had they mourned in vain, and long had they wept, when the man one day went to his wife and said:

"All this lamentation and sorrow are useless. Now we will try magic."

It was autumn. The earth had begun to freeze; fine snow, light, thin snow, covered the plains, and the nights began to grow long and dark.

Early one morning, just as the first gray dawn was show-ing itself, the man took his wife down to the beach by the sea. Here the man took a piece of flint and struck sparks all around them while he recited strange incantations. Then they went home. Four times they went down to the beach thus, when the earliest dawn was showing like a grayish cloudbank in the black sky, and each time the man per-formed his strange charms. When, after the fourth morn-ing, they returned home the man said to his wife, "Now we will have a son."

Not long after that the woman gave birth to a son.

The old Woodman had captured a wandering falcon in a net, and with its skin he washed the entire body of the in-fant. The falcon's skin became the boy's first amulet.

The mother had borne her child in a shelter outside the house; now she moved into a little tent, where she remained four days before she was allowed to return to the house which she shared with her husband. This was the custom with mothers in the old days.

The Woodman had big plans for the boy who one day was to avenge all their misfortune. He was called after his first amulet, which was a Wander-hawk; and the object of his life was, some day to go out over all the earth to pursue his quest. He came also to be called Qajartuarungnertoq, which means: "He who shall always long to go roaming in his kayak."

THE WOODMAN TRIES IN VAIN TO KILL HIS SON

THE old Woodman was always full of ideas and actions. The first thing he made for his wife, when she came home after the child's birth, was an *aqupivik*, a strange-looking resting log, a divided tree trunk, sharp and pointed underneath. It was difficult to hold one's balance on it, and as soon as she rose, it would fall to one side. She was never allowed to sit on anything else when she had the boy with her. For long before he attempted to walk he must learn how difficult it is to hold the body in perfect poise. He who lies on a broad and commodious bunk that is warm and makes him drowsy, is apt to get the idea that life is easy like that.

But the Woodman wished to make his son watchful and wakeful, otherwise he would never be able to avenge his brothers. A lazy and easy-going man does not fight against the wickedness of life and the treachery of men. And the old man knew that these were the things that made him childless in his old age. It was not the wild beasts of the forest that took his sons from him. And now the last-born was to be not merely powerful as a hunter, but also invulnerable, one whom no ignorance and no evil could surprise. Therefore he gathered amulets for him now, all kinds of small vermin and grubs of the sort that die in winter and wake up again in summer. Men should be like these insects, these midgets, beginning as grubs that lie torpid, but waking up as swift-winged, glittering, rainbow-hued fliers. So thought the Woodman, and his wife sewed larva after larva, swathed in skin, tight inside of the boy's fur coat. But besides all these tiny vermin that must not be despised, there were also sewn into his clothes skins of weasels, ermine, and field mice.

So the boy grew up under his father's constant supervision. Seldom was he left to himself; there were always unexpected surprises prepared for him; the father was cruel in his attention and quite brutal in his method of rearing him. It is told that when the boy was big enough to begin to walk, and for the first time toddled across the floor from the mother to the father, the father suddenly seized his knife and threw it with furious strength after the unsuspecting child. But swift as lightning, the child drew aside as if by chance, and avoided the knife. Time after time the father did the same thing, with the same result, and rejoiced to see that the child had the instinct of danger, that instinct which is the most important in life. The amulets did not fail, though the father tested them in all sorts of ways. One day when the boy lay asleep on the bunk, the father opened the window from outside and shot arrow after arrow against the sleeper. The boy moved in his sleep, and the arrows missed their mark; evidently hidden enemies, shooting from behind, would not harm him.

Wander-hawk was now allowed to run out and play. He hunted birds and small animals to the best of his ability, and showed great skill in slaying; thus he gave promise of some day becoming a good hunter.

Wander-Hawk's amulets did not fail.

One day he was playing on a plain near the house and found a little toy arrow which he knew did not belong to himself. He ran to his parents with it, showed it to them, and asked:

"What is that? Where did that come from? There are no other children here."

But the parents gave him no answer. He was still too young to understand, much too young to feel the flame of wrath. Another day he found a toy bow which had once been lost in the grass; this, too, did not belong to himself. Again he asked where it had come from and if there had been other children in his home. But again the parents said nothing of the brothers he had lost. They wished to put off telling him of their great sorrow, until the tale could impress him with the thought that he was born to avenge his brothers, that his whole existence centered in this vengeance.

Autumn came. Winter approached, and the family moved from the summer tent to the winter house. The father immediately set up all kinds of craftily devised snares for the boy, both outside the house and inside in the long dark passage. But the boy always shunned the dangers he met.

Then the father dug a pitfall in one of the places where the boy used to play, a pitfall covered with faggots and small twigs and invisible to those who did not know about it, a trap of the kind used for wolves and caribou, with sharp knives hidden in the bottom. Animals did not see it, noticed nothing—went over the loose branches that were laid over its opening in the ground, tumbled in and were

pierced by the knives. But the boy avoided all the pitfalls.
Here too the amulets worked.

WANDER-HAWK HEARS HIS STORY

WANDER-HAWK became a great hunter and trapper. And
one day, when he had grown old enough to understand seri-
ous things and to feel grief and anger, the father told him
about the four brothers who disappeared while hunting, who
were slain, murdered, obliterated from the earth in a way
which was never cleared up. The news made the boy silent,
and in silence he resolved to be the avenger of his brothers.

But the father was old and no longer much of a hunter,
and the mother, too, was feeble, so the son must first gather
food for his parents. Throughout the summer he hunted
white whale; in his kayak he drove them from the open sea
into shallow water where, terrified, they were caught fast
because they could not dive, and were easy to harpoon.
Flock after flock he drove in, and he amassed immense
quantities of meat. But all this meat could not be allowed
to rot, so he dug store chambers deep down in the frozen
ground, ice houses which could accommodate the meat and
blubber of the white whale and the bearded seal.

After this he hunted caribou and carried the booty down
to the old folks' dwelling. Sometimes he drove the animals
down living and killed them close to the house. Here he set
up high game gibbets made of ponderous tree trunks and

filled them with the meat of fat autumn deer; not one, but many game gibbets, some for meat, others for skins. And on the top of the shore cliffs he built, with a view over sea and land, a big wooden house for his old parents.

Wander-hawk had become restless and silent. One great thought obsessed him. But before leaving home he must thoroughly provide for those that were to stay behind. It seemed as if he would never have enough meat. Thin ice began to cover the sea while he was still hunting the white whale. He was never at rest for a single day; if not hunting, he was dragging animals down to his parents' huge store chambers, which had been dug like ice caverns deep in the ground. The first snow fell, and when it covered the ground he asked his father to make him a sledge. The mother sewed strong *kamiks* for him, and made all his clothing ready for a long journey. No one spoke of what was to happen, yet the father and mother knew that Wander-hawk was setting out to avenge his brothers. He himself was till the very last day busy gathering meat and setting all in order, so that the old folk should have enough of everything for a long, long time.

The father built the sledge, and the mother sewed; but she also filled the stomach of a white whale with delicious *akutaq*, which is a mixture of caribou's stomach, tallow, and fat; with magic words she put a spell on this food and made it sacred meat, of which he was to partake only when journeying through dangerous regions. A mouthful, or even quite a tiny piece, of a morning, would give him second sight for a day and make him aware of all that would happen that day.

The mother also set a wooden pot in his sledge, a *qajûtaq*, such as was used in the old days, a pot made out of a hollowed root or a hard bit of wood. It is filled with water and small round stones are warmed in a fire, till they sputter with heat; then they are laid in the pot. As soon as the stones cool off, they are exchanged for others, and this goes on till the water begins to boil. Then the meat is added, which tastes delicious prepared in this way. Thus was all made ready for the long journey.

WANDER-HAWK SETS OUT ON THE LONG TRAIL

ONE autumn day of still weather and cloudy sky Wander-hawk found himself at last ready for the road. The ground was nice and firm, easy to walk on, easy to draw a sledge on. His old parents remained a long time sitting outside their house looking after him; neither of them said anything, but when the lad was already some distance off, the father suddenly rose and called out, just as if he had all at once thought of something:

"May you have good weather till you meet your uncle."

Wander-hawk didn't know that he had an uncle. Where should he seek him? He had never heard of him. But he thought to himself, "Well, if I have an uncle, I'll surely meet him somewhere or other." And he turned round and waved to the old folk, so that they could see that he had understood them. Thereupon he set out on his long journey to avenge his brothers by warring against life's wickedness and men's treachery.

He went northward in the direction of the high mountains, and walked and walked, dragging his sledge after him.

Far inland he came in sight of a lake, a large inland lake he had never seen before. Here he heard men's voices, went on, and soon discovered a crowd of men who were carrying peat down to the lake. They were all busy dragging the peat and carrying it down to the lake. Whatever were they going to do with all that peat? He could not tell, and drew nearer, but nobody noticed him, nobody saw him, and so he went on without stopping.

He traveled and traveled and came to a deep gorge between the mountains in the uplands between Silivik and Kobuk. Here he set eyes on a man—a solitary man—sitting right out at the fringe of the wood. A man with his bow in one hand and arrows in the other. Arrows with sharp flint points; his quiver hung at his back. There sat the man and looked eagerly about on all sides, yet Wander-hawk passed close by him without the other seeing him and went on without stopping; he had no use for the man. So he went on day after day and met with remarkable adventures.

WANDER-HAWK MEETS A WOOD-PECKER IN A MAN'S SHAPE

ONE evening Wander-hawk chose a place to pitch his camp. He felled trees, built a shelter of small pines, spread a layer of branches on the ground, gathered wood, and lighted a big fire. Then he hunted ptarmigan for his supper and cooked them over the fire on a spit, sitting beside the fire.

But what was that? Suddenly there stood a man just outside! And he cried to him: "I thought I should be alone this evening! Hi! Come in and we will eat together."

A strange, unfriendly man it was who now came in. His eyes seemed always to be looking past things, and he did not look Wander-hawk in the face. But he was offered food, and they ate in silence. Wander-hawk became more and more angry with all this unfriendliness until, beside himself because of the other's taciturnity, he jumped over the fire, seized the silent fellow by the nape of the neck, and held him over the blaze so that the fringes of his furs were scorched. Thereupon he threw him high over the wind shelter, out on the snow beyond the camp fire. He listened for angry words, but all that he heard was a tapping sound, like someone knocking on a tree trunk. Shortly after, a woodpecker flitted up and flew off. A woodpecker in a man's shape had been his guest.

THE WOLVERINE THAT HAD
BROKEN A TOOTH

NEXT morning Wander-hawk continued his journey, following a river that led into a ravine. Here he discovered a
beavers' lodge, and when he examined it closely he saw by
the footprints in the snow that a wolverine had tried to rob
it. But the lodge had been too well built. The wolverine had
broken one of its large teeth and had run off with its purpose unaccomplished.

Wander-hawk enlarged the hole which the wolverine had
gnawed, and dragged out four young beavers which he killed.
Then he laid them on his sledge, covered them well so that
they could not freeze before he skinned them, and went on.
In the evening he pitched his camp on the outskirts of a
wood and fetched kindling to build a fire for the night. Then
he met a man with very fine *kamiks* and broad, richly ornamented shoulder trimmings, all of the finest wolverine skin.
The latter was a friendly, talkative man, an attractive man,
who helped to skin the fat, delicious young beavers, and
Wander-hawk took out his wooden pot, warmed stones over
the fire, and cooked the meat.

During the meal the stranger told that he, too, had tried
to hunt beavers, but had been unlucky enough to break his
valuable and rare jade ax.

Oh, how strong they both felt, how thoroughly satisfied!
The young tender meat seemed to permeate their whole
being, their tongues were loosened by it, and they chatted

cozily together. Wander-hawk began to tell about his beaver hunt, and that a wolverine had broken one of its big teeth on the same lodge that he had rifled.

At this the strange guest blurted out:

"What did the wolverine want there? A wolverine! What did the wolverine want there? A wolverine!" And he kept repeating this and said nothing else whatever for the rest of the evening. "What was the wolverine doing there? A wolverine!" Thus he went on repeating the very thing he wanted to hide.

Next morning, when Wander-hawk awakened, his guest was gone, and he saw the fresh spoor of a wolverine leading out from the camp. His guest had been a wolverine in the shape of a man. Just that very wolverine that had broken its tooth on the beavers' lodge.

THE FRIGHTENED LYNX, OR "WHAT DOES YOUR BIG TOE EAT?"

AFTER eating a little of his mother's magic food, Wander-hawk continued his journey. About midday his way took him across a mountain. The sun was warm, the snow soft and half thawed with the midday heat. His *kamiks* were wet through, and the seam of one of the feet had a small rip through which his big toe stuck out.

Ah! Just look! Here came a man! A man in white clothes.

The only dark part of his dress was the fine border of wolverine skin round his neck band. It was a lynx in the shape of a man. They met smiling, laughed together, and sat down on their sledges facing each other, clearing away the snow between them, and Wander-hawk offered the stranger beaver meat from yesterday's meal.

Suddenly the white stranger looked down at Wander-hawk's feet and noticed the big toe sticking out. For a while he gazed at it and then burst out, as if frightened:

"What does your big toe usually eat?"

"If I meet a stranger, it eats him."

"Hold on to it! Hold on to it!"

And the lynx gave a terrified spring high up into the air, while Wander-hawk held on to his leg. The lynx ran away, and Wander-hawk hopped about with one hand round his big toe, roaring with laughter, breathless with merriment. Then he threw his old *kamiks* away and put on another pair.

THE FOOL WHO THREW HIMSELF INTO THE FIRE

WANDER-HAWK went through a gorge and over some low hills and toward evening met a man dragging a sledge.

They cleared away the snow between the sledges and ate beaver meat together. There seemed to be no limit to the stranger's appetite. He ate and ate very fast, and when there was no more beaver meat he said suddenly:

"You look as if you would be a tasty man, let me eat you, too."

With that he jumped up, seized his knife, and ran after Wander-hawk. The latter had no desire to do him any harm right away, and both began to run round the sledges. Wander-hawk was very nimble, the other could not get near him. At last Wander-hawk ran up to a tree with a cloven trunk and began to run round it. The other ran after him, and they went on with this until at last the stranger gave up and jumped down to his sledge. From this he took a bird snare, hastened back to the tree, and set up the snare. Meanwhile Wander-hawk had climbed the tree and now watched him from this perch, at the same time filling his inner vest with small twigs. When the other tried to force Wander-hawk into the snare he threw his vest in, jumped up into a tree beside it, and looked on. His trick was successful and the stranger seized the stuffed vest in the belief that it was the man himself.

"So he wasn't to be caught and so he escaped, did he?" cried the stranger mockingly, believing that it was the man himself he had caught. He took the vest carefully out of the snare, cleared a camping place, fetched wood, and lighted a fire. Wander-hawk sat in the tree and laughed. When the fire was burning well and the flames were roaring high, the stranger fetched a knife from his sledge and fell to skinning the vest.

"You are a fool and you act like a fool," Wander-hawk now cried down to him, and when the other looked up he added:

"Cut your throat and throw yourself into your own fire."

Immediately the fool gave himself a cut in the throat and cast himself into his own camp fire. Fools are like that: they don't know what they do; they are simple-hearted and act like simpletons. But Wander-hawk let himself gently down from the tree, took his vest, shook all the small twigs out of it, and put it on. Then he went out to his sledge and continued his wanderings.

ANOTHER FOOL, WHO HANGED HIMSELF IN HIS SLEDGE HARNESS

Wander-hawk traveled and traveled and came to stony and steep mountains on which there grew a few solitary spruce.

That evening he wanted to be undisturbed, and chose a camping ground at the foot of a steep slope, a place from which his camp fire could be easily seen from all sides. But he liked to play tricks on people. So he did not take the direct way down to the place he had chosen, but fastened a rope round his sledge and let it run down the dangerous slope, drawing it carefully back again upon its own tracks. And now he took an easy detour round the back of the slope down to the place where he was to sleep, and lighted his fire for the night. Everyone who saw the camp fire would now think that the way led down the steep declivity. And indeed it was not long before he heard a voice which kept on repeating just these words:

"By what way did you get down to your camping place?"

"Don't you see my tracks?"

The man only noticed the tracks which went straight down over the slope and could not see that the sledge had been drawn back again the same way.

"Can one follow them?"

"You can easily follow them."

So the noise was heard of the man's snowshoes, and then suddenly came a cry for help.

"Help! Help! Help!"

"Yes! I'll just put something on my feet."

But it was the tongue only that said this. Wander-hawk did not stir from his seat, and a moment after all was still again.

Next morning Wander-hawk found a strange man dead, hanging in his own sledge harness. He had tried to drive down the slope on one side of a tree, a solitary tree that stood in the center of the cliff, but the heavy sledge had taken the other side of the tree, and so it had happened that the stranger remained hanging in his sledge harness without being able to get up or down. He could have slipped out of the harness, but he had not thought of that. He, too, was a fool.

WANDER-HAWK WEDS A NIGHT OWL

ON WENT Wander-hawk, on over the mountains until he came in sight of Kobuk River, near the place which is called the "Lip Ornament."

"Men in the underwood. Smoke," said Wander-hawk to himself.

Smoke was rising.

"There must be a house down there," he thought, and went down. It was evening before he reached the settlement. There was a house; a house with two game gibbets. These indicated that good hunters dwelt here. He put his sledge aside and went forward.

Folk came to meet him, a young man and two young girls. They all received him kindly and set food before him: the shoulder blades and a bit of the foreleg of a rabbit. Oh, dear! It was such a tiny little fragment of meat they offered him, and he ate it all up! The people of the place looked on astounded, and at last the old father of the house said:

"Glutton! Glutton!"

Wander-hawk pretended not to hear, they were otherwise so friendly, and so he settled down with them and took the youngest woman as his wife. After that he lived there but never went hunting. All that he did was to eat in company with his house mates. They never ate anything but rabbits, and only tiny little rabbits at that. The old father-in-law often sighed in despair:

"If we're to have this glutton living with us very long we'll starve to death before the winter is out."

But Wander-hawk pretended not to hear. At last the winter was over, spring came, and the sun rose high in the heavens. The people of the settlement had the remarkable custom of going hunting only at night. Wander-hawk's young brother-in-law used to set off in the evening and come back towards morning. His clothing was often covered with blood, but he never brought any meat along. The women had to go and get it. They skinned the small rabbits just as if they had been real beasts of prey, carried them home, and laid them on the game gibbets outside the house. Meanwhile the hunter lay indoors on the bunk and rested, just as if he had been out after regular big game, and he went to sleep, exhausted.

Wander-hawk had married into a family of night owls. They could not see during the day and so they only hunted at night.

But one day Wander-hawk awakened. He had had enough of idling, and to his house mates' great amazement he set off hunting in the middle of the day. It was clear weather, and the sun shone on the far-away, bluish mountains when Wander-hawk fastened on his snowshoes. But his house mates tumbled down on their beds, dazzled by the bright light.

Wander-hawk did not stay away long, and yet he had as many rabbits as he could carry when he came back. The night owls thronged about him in astonishment and stared with wonder at his mighty catch. Then he built a great fire, gathered wood in huge piles, and roasted the rabbits on a spit, one to each person in the house; he himself ate as many as he was able to, and when at last he was satisfied he hung up the rest on the game gibbet. Then he called his wife and said:

"I cannot settle down, for I am out to avenge my brothers. May you soon have a son who can hunt for you."

These were Wander-hawk's farewell words, and thereupon he continued his long journey.

THE GIANT WHO WAS SO BIG THAT HIS NIGHT WAS A WHOLE WINTER

WANDER-HAWK went on and on until one day he reached the big river Noatak. He followed its course up country and came to some high cliffs where he found a number of dead caribou. There lay caribou upon caribou one on top of the other! He investigated the place, found something that looked like a rift in the snow, and caught a glimpse far, far down of something that resembled a man. He poked it a little with his stick but could not discover what it was and went on his way again. A crowd of foxes, wolves, and wolverines hung about the place and ate the caribou, and Wander-hawk at once began to catch wolf and wolverine. He caught many, flayed them, and dried the fine skins.

Spring came. The sun began to melt the snow. Moss appeared. The air was warm.

One day Wander-hawk saw a powerful man squatting on the ground in the melting snow, a huge man. Wander-hawk went up to him, but the giant did not see him or take the slightest notice of him although Wander-hawk kept on going round him. At last he climbed up the giant's leg and ran to and fro right before his nose; then the giant discovered him and said smilingly:

"Dear little child, how do you come here?"

Wander-hawk told about his journey; the giant yawned now and then, stretched his arms wearily, and seemed quite sleepy. Afterwards Wander-hawk learned that he had lain down to sleep late in the summer, towards autumn. The winter was his night, so big was he, and he hadn't noticed in the least that the snow had covered him. It was too insignificant for him to feel; he had only awakened now when it was thawing.

"Aha! You little fellow!" said the giant. "Let us go down to my house."

A house! Oh! There was such a big, big house! Wander-hawk had often seen it while hunting wolf and wolverine, but he had thought that it was a cliff, a mountain wall.

The giant rose and stretched himself. When his warm breath struck a lake, the ice broke up, and a foaming mountain river dashed over the cliff. Then he shook his bedding, and at once a storm rose and swept away the last remains of the snow. They then set off in company to the house.

Oh! It was a mountain wall, a mountain, nay, mountains. And they went into the immense house where caribou hung in bunches under the roof like small birds. But the giant wanted fresh meat and went hunting. He had no bow and arrow, but only a *bola* of the kind used for bird-catching. When he came back, many caribou hung round his belt like rabbits or other small game.

The giant was a good man and always friendly to Wander-hawk; they lived happily together and grew fond of each other. But when the water began to gather in the crevices and the summer was well begun, the giant became restless and anxious and worried. Now he explained that he had two wives. One lived in the woods, the other by the sea. They usually visited him on the same day, running a race with each other. Then he had a hard day, for the women were very jealous and neither of them would allow the other to be first; they were both just as big as himself, and they fought over him and made him suffer from their jealousy.

At some distance from his house there was a plain be-tween two mountains; there the battle for him usually took place. The giant, who was otherwise afraid of nothing in the world, trembled before his wives and begged Wander-hawk to help him. He gave him a knife so big that Wander-hawk could scarcely lift it, and said:

"As usual, they will both hurl themselves upon me with their caresses. Then you must hamstring them with this knife, to weaken them."

The giant had acquired great respect for little Wander-hawk. He had seen him drive many caribou down to their house and kill them with bow and arrow. The giant had a *kukuvfak*—a blunt arrow such as men use for ptarmigan, where the arrowhead is merely a blunt end without point.

The arrow he used for caribou was a great spruce trunk where the root itself formed the blunt end, and when he shot this arrow into a flock it killed many caribou and whirled them away like a storm.

At last, one morning, the giant got ready for his visitors. He put on his old clothes and looked now toward the sea and now toward the woods. The wife from the sea was the first to be seen, running breathlessly, the wind whistling in her clothing like a storm. But the wife from the woods came running just as violently. Both were longing for their man and threw themselves upon him; they tumbled over him like a landslide, and neither of them could endure to have the other come first. Thus they wrestled on the plain between the two mountains, and the wretched giant groaned under the weight of their enormous caresses. Then Wander-hawk came to the rescue with his big two-bladed knife; it was more ax than knife—he could hardly lift it—but he hacked as well as he could, hamstringing the raging women so that their legs grew weak and they had to lie down. There they lay on the plain, worn out, resting, and only then did the giant get breath. All day they remained lying there on the plain.

The two women had brought a great many clothes with them, each had her mighty load on her back, which was now placed on the gibbet for skins outside the house. And now came the giant, friendly as ever, and asked Wander-hawk what use he would make of his numerous skins of wolf and wolverine.

"They are for anyone who has a use for them," answered Wander-hawk.

The giant was pleased and gave his wives strips for their fur coats, the finest any woman could wish for. When it was evening, the two giantesses went back, one to the woods, the other to the sea. The giant was greatly relieved. Now a whole year would elapse before they would visit him again.

Wander-hawk struck up a warm friendship with the giant and sought to please him in many ways. One day, while the giant was out hunting, Wander-hawk split up marrow bones. There was a great heap of caribou bones which had been thrown into a corner of the giant's house. These he split and packed the fat marrow in a caribou's stomach, and when the giant came home and lay down on his bed, Wander-hawk cried to him: "Open!" And thereupon he popped the whole thing into his mouth. Oh! What a dainty tidbit! The giant had never before tasted such a thing. He never dreamed such a fine dish was to be had from the bones of a small animal.

Wander-hawk remained with the giant throughout three of his days, that is, for three years, and when the giant lay down to rest for the fourth winter, he set out again on his long journey. He knew that if the giant suspected he was going to forsake him, he would never get leave to do so, so fond of each other had they grown.

ALL THE WOODLAND CREATURES
BUILD A BIRCH-BARK CANOE
FOR WANDER-HAWK

WANDER-HAWK went on, far across country. He followed a deep ravine and was soon so far to the south that the snow began to melt; he was in the neighborhood of the Indians' country, and here he chased caribou and killed many of them, seeking out those that he thought would have the best marrow bones. Then he loaded his sledge with fine, delicious fat meat and dragged it down to the big river called Yukon. Here he must build a kayak to get over the river, but how should he get hold of skin for it? He tried the forest trees, cutting off their bark to find out which was lightest and floated best, and he discovered that the bark of a birch tree was the one best suited for covering a kayak. So he sought out a big birch tree, cut its bark in pieces shaped like hides, and felled spruce, which he split. Then he cleared a good camping ground on the fringes of the wood, felled trees, built wind screens, and lighted a big fire. His caribou meat he left on the sledge some distance from the fire, and lay down in the warmth of the blaze wishing with all his might that men might come along who would like to eat all his delicious meat and in return would help him to build a kayak. With these thoughts he fell asleep beside the fire.

Towards morning he awakened and heard men's voices around him. Their talking aroused him, and when he looked around he saw crowds of people. One might really think

they were fulfilling some appointment. They were all work-
ing on his kayak, some making the framework, others the
side ribs; all were busy with the various parts of the kayak.
Some distance from the men young girls were cooking meat,
the meat of his caribou. Thus everything he wished for
had come to pass. All the animals of the woodland had
come to him in the shape of men, and now they were helping
him to build a kayak.

The wood squirrel collected fir cones and boiled resin
from them, to be smeared over the stitching. Strange-looking birds with long bills gathered the bark. They made sewing
thread of the roots of the young spruce, which they split
into thin strands. It was not a real kayak they were building, but a birch-bark canoe which was open at the top. The
bark was sewed together for a cover, and the hedgehog
smeared resin over the seams. The beaver was a carpenter
and cut the tree, sawed it up with his sharp teeth, and fitted
the pieces together. He also cut a fine oar and made a harpoon, while the raven labored over the bird bolt and wooden
javelin.

All the woodland creatures were assembled: red foxes,
wolves, wolverines, bears, ermines, lynxes, weasels, long-
legged cranes, and high-necked swans; and they all ate the
meat which the young girls cooked. It was lively and festive
in the wood. Only the beaver, the squirrel, and the hedgehog
did not eat with them, for they do not like meat.

Wander-hawk lay awake and watched happily how the
work advanced. By the time the sun was risen above the
horizon and beginning to give warmth, the canoe was built

and covered. The woodland creatures had built a fine canoe in a single night. Wander-hawk gazed at all the pretty young girls and was seized with a desire to capture one of them. Suddenly he jumped up and threw himself upon them, and he caught the prettiest of them all, a sweet little red fox.

But this frightened the others, who began to tumble over each other helter-skelter, becoming animals again. Some spread their wings and rose into the air; others fell forward and ran on all fours into the wood; others threw themselves into the river. Only the little red vixen struggled in vain to be free. But Wander-hawk talked caressingly to her and calmed her.

"I want to hear a voice near me, the voice of a talking human being—I want to have a comrade while I am waiting for the river to clear. It is spring, and the ice has just broken up. The stream still runs too fiercely, the current is too rapid, and the canoe will be difficult to steer. You shall stay with me while I am waiting, and I will not harm you."

She stayed with him while he waited for the river's course to slacken. In memory of her former kin she always wore a red inner fur. He whiled away the time with hunting and collected much meat, which the vixen dried for him.

But one morning he discovered that the water of the river had gone down and was running clear; the current was as it should be; so he decided to set out. He ate a little of his mother's charmed meat and gave the young woman all the meat he had collected. That was his thanks because she had stayed with him. And so the fox and her family received all his huge catch; and they came out and busied themselves carrying it away to their hiding places.

But Wander-hawk took to his canoe and floated down the river.

WANDER-HAWK MEETS HIS UNCLE

ONE day he came sailing past some hillocks, and on the top of one of them sat a man, a solitary man, staring at the canoe which the current was bearing at full speed down toward him.

He looked like a man who was out strolling, for all he had with him were the gloves he was sitting on and a ladle with a wooden handle which he used to chase away the midges. He was a man from the woods.

Wander-hawk called to him:

"Uncle! Come down and let's travel together!"

The lonely man rose at once as if he had only sat up there on the hill and waited for someone to come, and sat down in the canoe with his back to his nephew. Wander-hawk arranged the seat on a layer of bark, over which he spread rugs of the neck skin of two caribou. Uncle must have a soft seat. So they floated farther down the river. For a long while they were silent. Wander-hawk was the first to speak:

"Uncle, tell me, isn't there anything you would like to eat? Something you have felt the want of up here in the woods and which you are now longing for?"

His uncle answered: "Maybe young bearded seals."

Immediately a young striped seal rose in front of the canoe. Wander-hawk harpooned it, and they went ashore to cook it. They lighted a fire, warmed stones, and put them into the wooden pot.

Wander-hawk spoke again, saying:

"Uncle, fill the pot with the pieces you like best."

And so they cooked the daintiest bits of striped seal, while Wander-hawk told about his parents who lived down at Silivik, and about his four brothers who had disappeared. Now he was out to avenge them, which he would do by killing everything hostile and dangerous that crossed his way. He would uproot malice and all kinds of secret evil; yes, everything that threatened peaceful traveling; but toward good people he would be friendly, and would help them as well as he could. Thus Wander-hawk told about his life while they sat comfortably by the camp fire. The next day they sailed farther downstream.

THE MAN WHO MAKES SALMON FOR HUMAN BEINGS

ONE day they came to a place where the river took a wide bend; here there was a bay, a lake with slack current, and by the bay stood a man, hacking with an ax into the trunks of the spruce trees. He stood there splitting one chip after another from the trunks, and it was impossible to see why he was doing it, for all the splinters of the trunks fell into the river; it looked like idle labor, since none fell on land.

Wander-hawk steered his boat nearer to the place where the man was standing, and said to his uncle:

"Just look at that man there, who stands and toils to no earthly purpose."

"A-ah!" shouted the man from the land—he seemed to have very sharp hearing—"I'm making salmon for men."

Wander-hawk rowed nearer to the man, who was steadily hacking chips and splinters out of a tree trunk, and now he saw that the chips disappeared in the stream in the strangest way, vanishing in the foam and eddies. He looked closer and discovered that it was really as the man said. Every single time a tree splinter fell into the river it became alive—it became a trout or a salmon, flipping its tail and vanishing in the depths. This remarkable man was the salmon's father.

THE STICKY BALL

ON GLIDED Wander-hawk and his uncle down the river, and while they sat in the canoe and let the current carry them onward, Wander-hawk said to his uncle as usual:

"What is your favorite food in the fall? Is there nothing you've a special fancy for?"

"Yes. A mountain ram."

Scarcely had his uncle said the word when they saw a large ram on the land. Wander-hawk at once steered his canoe towards the bank and shot the beast with his bow.

Then they pitched their camp, lighted a fire, gathered the tallow and the inner fat, cooked the meal, and feasted on the dainty meat. They dried the skin which would be used to sleep on.

Next morning Wander-hawk took a little mouthful of his mother's magic food, and they set off again and sailed farther down the river. At some distance they caught sight of a ball, a big round ball hanging on a cord between two trees.

Wander-hawk grew curious, let his uncle stay in the canoe, and went up to examine the ball more closely.

"A queer hunting tool," he said, touching it with one hand.

Immediately his hand stuck to it; he tried to strike the ball away with his other hand, but that, too, stuck fast, and he could not get it loose. Then he tried to kick the ball, first with one foot and then with the other, but now his feet, too, clung to it, and he was dangling in the air. Here he hung all day, and nothing happened until toward evening he heard a shout: "At last something is caught in my snare!"

Out from the wood came a man with dark skin and hairy face. He touched Wander-hawk, who, however, made himself stiff with magic words, and the man from the woods, who thought that his prey had been dead for some time, took him down, threw him over his shoulder, and went up through the wood, following a path. Along the path grew small trees, and Wander-hawk took hold of these, so that the man must stop. The man of the woods could not understand what was the matter; he laid his burden down, examined it, and tickled it to see if there were life in it; but it seemed dead and stiff.

His wife saw him coming and called from a long distance:
"Look! Look! To-day Father has caught something."
The children came out and ran to meet him, shouting:
"Father! Father! Nice kidney fat for me!"

But the father was tired and laid his booty on a platform beside the fire. Wander-hawk thought: "If only they would put an ax under my head." And immediately the man said to his wife:

"Put an ax under his head."

A little later they moved him to the place under the little window way above the fireplace where they were in the habit of thawing the meat. Here Wander-hawk ventured to open his eyes a little and look about him. But one of the boys discovered it and cried:

"Father! Father! He's opening his eyes!" But the father laughed and treated it as a joke.

Now Wander-hawk wanted to turn his head a little to look about the house, and happened to make a face. Immediately the boy shouted:

"Father! Father! He's making faces!" But once more the father turned it off as a joke, saying, "He's looking about to see whom I shall catch next."

All the corners of the house were full of men's bones that had been gnawed and chewed. It was a regular man-slayer's house, this, a man-slayer's and man-eater's house.

In the evening they lay down to sleep. But scarcely had they lain down when Wander-hawk sprang up and killed them all with the marrow-bone hammer he had had put under his head: first the father, then the mother, and afterwards the boys. Then he took the path back to the river, but passed the ball on the way, and lo, it was no longer sticky! It had lost its power now that the magician was dead. Then he went down to his uncle, who was still sitting there in the canoe waiting.

"What would you have a fancy for now, Uncle?"

"Goslings."

Immediately goslings swam out from the river banks, and Wander-hawk killed as many as he could. They found a sheltered place on the edge of the wood, where they cleared a camping ground. Here they slept, after having made a meal off the tender, fat goslings.

THE KAYAK WIZARD'S DANGER-OUS MAN TRAP

EARLY in the morning Wander-hawk, as usual, ate a little of his mother's magic food and then put on his amulet shirt, for to-day he expected greater difficulties than usual. Then they again drifted down the river with the current. Soon they heard a booming noise ahead of them, which increased gradually as they came nearer, and now they came in sight of two steep cliffs which jutted out from either bank of the river, opening and shutting like a big mouth that is chewing. Every time they closed all the water of the river foamed into mighty whirlpools.

Wander-hawk had to paddle to and fro all the time, keeping in uninterrupted motion so as not to be swallowed in the maelstrom; the mountains' mighty sluice gates penned up the great river-flood in a boiling cauldron. At last he said: "Uncle, shut your eyes." Then he began a magic song:

> *"Travel will I free and scatheless*
> *Twixt these precipices narrow,*
> *Lips against each other biting!"*

Immediately the cliffs opened, and the canoe slipped through, but so quickly did the rocks shut again after them, that they cut off the point of the stern.

They sailed farther downstream till they caught sight of a huge tree trunk laid across the river; it was in constant motion and lashed the river with mighty force. Wander-hawk sang no magic song here, but rowed right up to the trunk and slipped past just as it was rising.

Now they glided onward swiftly through the rapid and foaming river. Suddenly they set eyes on a kayak that was coming to meet them—a huge kayak such as the Indians use. As soon as the man in the kayak saw the canoe coming down the current he cried:

"It must be difficult to get the better of you two, since you have come through my trap alive. Now it is my turn to test you."

"Uncle! Do you think we shall get the better of him?" whispered Wander-hawk.

The giant had a big bird harpoon with a javelin, and while

he recited a magic song, he seized his bird dart and threw it;
but he missed his aim, for at the same moment Wander-
hawk dodged to the side with his canoe. Now it was Wander-
hawk who seized his bird dart, sang a magic song, and cast.
The bird dart tore off one of the giant's arms. Now the giant
took a turn. Again he missed his aim for Wander-hawk was
not where the other expected him to be, and in the next
round the giant lost his other arm. In vain he now attempted
to hold his harpoon with his mouth, for before he succeeded
Wander-hawk had again harpooned him, so that he overturned and drowned. Then the canoe sailed on and came to
a big chief's house, warm and well built. Inside the house
an old woman was lying. When she saw Wander-hawk, she
seized a little woman's knife and threw it after him, singing
the same magic song as the giant. But it turned out with
her as it had with her husband: she, too, was killed. The
people who lived here were goblins and when Wander-hawk
tried to leave the house, the passage closed before him.
However, he found a little rift, slipped out through it like a
mouse, in a mouse's shape, and thus came scatheless back to
his uncle.

WANDER-HAWK TEASES AN UN-FRIENDLY SALMON FISHER

ON THEY went down the river. Toward evening, when it was
time to think of a camping place, Wander-hawk said as

usual to his uncle: "Isn't there anything you have a fancy for? Anything you remember from your winter hunting?"

"Yes," said his uncle. "A fat caribou bull."

A moment later they saw a caribou on the river bank. Wander-hawk shot it with his bow, and they pitched their camp for the night.

Afterwards they ate all kinds of tidbits from the caribou, spending much time cooking it, and remaining there some days. The place was full of hostile folk, folk whose only thought was to kill.

One day, as he was going through a gorge, Wander-hawk caught sight of a man who stood catching salmon trout in a little brawling stream, stabbing at the passing trout with his fish spear.

Wander-hawk had a trout amulet, and now he threw himself into the river and swam slowly down to the fisherman, who saw him and grew excited. The man threw his fish spear after him, but he seized it and drew out its middle barb. Then he swam back, turned into a man again, and now came walking down to the trout fisher. The latter stood dazed and puzzled over his spear, which had lost its middle barb—he could not understand how. Wander-hawk offered to mend it for him, seized the fish spear, and to the man's great astonishment fastened the old barb on it again. The stranger looked on gaping, and could not understand how a strange man had got hold of the barb; but now Wander-hawk drove the spear right into the face of the wicked salmon fisher and threw him into the river. Then he went back to his uncle, and they sailed on down the stream.

WANDER-HAWK LETS HIMSELF BE EATEN BY THE CHIEF'S SON

ON THEY went gliding downstream.

"Uncle, isn't there anything you have a fancy for? Isn't there anything you've a craving to eat?"

"Yes. The skin and meat of a white whale."

Immediately a white whale rose in front of the canoe, and Wander-hawk harpooned it. Then they landed, flayed the whale, cooked and ate and rowed on.

Now they came to a place with low steep banks of clay. There was a narrowing in the river, and right across it from bank to bank a salmon net was stretched.

Wander-hawk anchored the canoe with his uncle on board, sprang on shore himself, and followed a path into the wood; here he saw many houses. Without making himself known, he went again down to the salmon net, sprang into the river, and by changing himself into the trout which was his amulet, let himself be caught in the net. In the afternoon the children of the settlement came down to look after the nets, and the chief's son captured Wander-hawk. It was the first salmon trout the chief's little son had caught and there was much shouting and gladness. According to custom and practice the fish must be cut up into many small pieces, dealt out to all houses, and be tasted by all. The chief's small son must have the head, he must suck the fat out of the delicate neck. But a bone stuck in his throat, and he died. At the same moment Wander-hawk sprang out of the corpse and became a human being again. There was great uproar. All shot arrows after him, but none hit him. He escaped to his canoe, where he met his uncle, and they sailed on again, down the river.

UNCLE CHANGES HIMSELF INTO A LYNX AND GOES OFF WITHOUT SAYING FAREWELL

THEY glided down the river through hill country. The land grew lower and lower; they came down to regular lowland, and the river was so muddy that it was difficult to travel. Suddenly they heard before them the cry of the sea; they heard a roaring which grew and grew the nearer they came, and when they were almost at the mouth of the river, they pitched their camp. There was still deep water in midchannel, but the banks were muddy with shallow water. They got ready for the night, and Wander-hawk wondered why his uncle had grown so quiet. He looked perturbed and unhappy, and Wander-hawk thought that the buffeting of the sea had tired him and was the cause of his silence. They lay down to sleep.

Next morning Uncle was gone—nowhere to be found—vanished!

Wander-hawk went up over the clay banks and looked for tracks. It was now early autumn and a light snow had fallen during the night. He found tracks that led towards the woods, and followed them. And lo, the human foot-prints suddenly changed to the trail of a lynx! Uncle had turned into a lynx and had forsaken him.

Then great grief overcame Wander-hawk, and he went slowly back to the camp. On the way he lamented aloud and could not restrain his tears; it was as if his mind had become darkened; and, weeping, he upbraided his uncle for leaving him without farewell, for turning back to the woods without a single word.

"And I did all I could to make him happy. I gave him all the meat he liked best at his mere wish. And yet he abandons me without a single word!"

Wander-hawk took his uncle's disappearance so much to heart that he decided to abandon his canoe and all he possessed at the mouth of the large river. He had now become accustomed to traveling along with his kinsman and had no desire to row farther alone. He hid his mother's wooden pot and his bow and arrow in a tree. Only his sleeping skins did he take with him and a pair of *kamiks,* and so made ready to start. He changed his shape, he no longer wished to be a man, but became a Wander-hawk, soaring high into the air and setting off again upon his long journey; for he had to travel all round the world.

WANDER-HAWK IS EATEN BY A CHIEFTAIN AND IS AFTERWARDS MARRIED TO HIS STEPDAUGHTER

Now he flew over the flat land with many lakes, the country between the Yukon and Norton Sound. Before he had gone far he saw houses—many houses; and near the houses, strange tall posts, inviting to rest on. He alighted on the tallest of the posts and from here examined the settlement. Then he heard people shouting:

"There's a wander-hawk in the snare! A wander-hawk in the chief's bird snare!"

"Oh," he thought, "then it's a bird snare I've sat down on." Such a snare he had never seen before; but now, when he tried to fly away, he found himself caught in a noose which tightened around him. People came running up, overthrew the post and took him out of the snare. The chief himself killed him and carried him to a gibbet where he used to hang his bird catch. Wander-hawk was fully conscious and only wanted to be eaten quickly, for through his amulets he had been given the magic power that as soon as he was eaten he came to life again as a human being. And he wished with all his might:

"If only the chief would take it into his head to eat me right away! If only I might be eaten at once!"

Scarcely had he thought this than the chief began to feel him.

"Ah-ha! A fine fat wander-hawk," he said. "Best to eat him at once."

And he took the bird home with him and gave it to a young girl who was to pluck it, cook it, and bring it to the feast house.

The young girl prepared the delicious bird and carried it on a wooden tray to the chief, who ate it at once. After the meal he asked the young girl to throw the bones out on the midden, and at the same instant Wander-hawk became a man again. He followed the young girl, who was no other than the chief's stepdaughter, into their house. All wondered who the young man might be who had turned up so suddenly. No one had seen him come. Wander-hawk looked quite unconcerned, settled down in the chief's house, and took his stepdaughter as his wife.

But this caused great ill-feeling between himself and the chief, for the latter had taken a fancy to his stepdaughter himself, and now he tried in all possible ways to murder his stepson.

FATHER-IN-LAW RAISES A STORM TO DESTROY WANDER-HAWK

THE chief had a big house which was filled with all kinds of good food. There were caribou meat, birds, and white whales. Many men lived at the settlement, and Wander-hawk eagerly took part in the hunting on sea and on land.

One morning his father-in-law, who was lying on the bunk fully dressed, legs outward, head in, seemed to be struggling with gloomy thoughts and said:

"One gets dainty. I've a craving to eat fresh birds like those caught in the snare."

And he told Wander-hawk that far, far out in the sea there were many eiderducks, so many that if a man just went out there he could fill his kayak.

Wander-hawk was immediately seized with a desire to go eiderduck hunting and made ready, putting on two storm jackets, one on top of the other, two rough-weather jackets of seal gut. Then he rowed out into the still, calm sea. He rowed and rowed, far, far out to sea.

The mountains began to separate; so far out did he go that they no longer formed a continuous chain, only the highest peaks could be seen, with nothing between. They were like a broken string. He had now reached the waters where the eiderduck abode.

And here indeed were eiderducks! The water was quite thick with them, and he filled his kayak both fore and aft, piling them up above each other; not till the boat was nearly sinking did he decide to row home. Scarcely was he under way when he heard a roaring, a strange far roaring. A storm arose from shore, the wind was like a thick darkness that came scurrying over the sea. So wild was the storm that Wander-hawk thought, "I wonder if this is to be the death of me!"

The tempest approached swiftly. Already the first whirl-winds were stirring the water as if it were boiling. Then

Wander-hawk remembered his amulets, the storm quellers;
these were two small round stones, a white one and a black
one, which his father had warmed in a fire till they were
simply spurting with white-hot sparks. It was just after
he was born, and he had to swallow them, and with a sound
like that of water poured on embers they slipped down into
his stomach. They were storm quellers which were still inside of him. Now he gulped them up, first one and then the
other, and blew them from him, saying:

"Don't stop, but burn through the storm till you come to
its source."

Away seethed the stones through the raging sea. A dead
calm followed in their path, and Wander-hawk rowed slowly,
at his ease, towards land.

But on the beach stood his father-in-law, blowing through
one of his sleeves; he stood there blowing weather and wind,
tempest and storm over the sea, with one arm out of its
sleeve so that he could blow through the armhole. His head
was wrapped up in his fur hood; he was full of ardor and
saw nothing; he just blew and blew—wind! wind! wind!

Suddenly first one and then the other glowing stone rushed
through his armhole and scorched all the skin off his face.
Then they turned back to Wander-hawk, who merely opened
his mouth and swallowed them.

Home he went with his kayak full of eiderducks, and told
cheerfully about his great haul. But Father-in-law was lying
in bed sick and scorched in his face, wicked and silent with
impotent wrath.

FATHER-IN-LAW TRIES TO KILL WANDER-HAWK WITH A TREE TRAP

FOR many, many days the whole settlement lived upon birds, almost until the burns on Father-in-law's face were healed. But one morning he was again lying upon the bunk, looking like a man who wants to say something.

"I wonder if our son-in-law would like to split fuel?"

Yes. Wander-hawk would gladly do so, and he was told that a long way up where the mountains end there was a big tree trunk which was to be cut up. Outside the house lay a stone wedge that he could use for splitting it. Wander-hawk followed Father-in-law's directions and easily found the tree trunk. It was thick and very heavy, and there were marks of a stone wedge in it. It looked as if others had tried to cleave it, without success. He thought: "I wonder if it isn't a trap for me." And he discovered that the tree trunk suddenly moved if a weight passed over it. It was so balanced that it fell upon whoever tried to split it. Wander-hawk passed his hand over it. This had a magic effect on it, and now he could quickly divide it into two portions with a mighty blow. It was now quite harmless, and he chopped it up into kindling wood. Then he went slowly homeward, taking things leisurely on the way. There was no hurry. He had discovered human skeletons beside the tree trunk and knew that his father-in-law had sent him out to meet the same death as all the others who had been there. On his return home he surprised his father-in-law, who was holding a song festival in the feast house, certain that he had succeeded in murdering the son-in-law, of whom he was constantly jealous. Wander-hawk went in quietly and told him that the trunk was cut up into kindling wood. Father-in-law's face was a study! And strangely enough no one was ever sent out to fetch the wood.

THE GIANT PTARMIGAN

ONE morning a long time afterwards, the house awakened again to find Father-in-law lying turned around on the bunk with his clothes on.

"I wonder if Son-in-law would like to go hunting?"

Yes, Wander-hawk would gladly do so, and Father-in-law now told him about a giant ptarmigan said to live at some distance up in the mountains. Wander-hawk was immediately seized with a desire to hunt it, and after directions from Father-in-law he wandered out in the early gray morning, following the mountains to a ravine where there was a coppice. He entered it and saw a ptarmigan: a huge, powerful giant ptarmigan lying on the outskirts of the thicket. It looked about, and when it set eyes on a man, stretched its neck, but immediately Wander-hawk changed himself into a little ermine that glided across the snow into the thicket, and the ptarmigan was reassured and began to nibble the bushes. Quite close beside the ptarmigan Wander-hawk again dived up from the snow and now aimed with his bow at the boneless place in the abdomen from which the heart can most easily be hit. He shot off his arrow, and the ptarmigan sprawled in its death agony, so that stones flew about his ears; it flapped its wings till there arose about him a whistling of wind and blizzard and then fell dead to the ground.

Later Wander-hawk examined the place and found many human bones and bows and arrows lying around. Father-in-law was a regular assassin, one of the kind that sends folk into an ambush to murder them, an evil man of the type Wander-hawk was out to combat. So he went slowly home, as if nothing had happened. Father-in-law, who was this time perfectly certain that he had killed his son-in-law, was again holding a song contest in the feast house. Wander-hawk went quietly in, and suddenly all was quiet,.as quiet as death.

WANDER-HAWK FIGHTS WITH THE SCALY MONSTER

IT WAS summer. Big hunting was afoot, and Wander-hawk was as usual collecting a great deal of meat for the house. He hunted caribou on land and eiderduck, speckled seal, young striped seal, and white whale on the water. A long time passed before Father-in-law again attempted to send him out on a death chase. But one morning the older man lay again turned round on the bunk, head inward, feet outward.

"Has Son-in-law a fancy to go hunting?"

Yes. Wander-hawk had that always. And so Father-in-law told the following:

Far inland, in the direction where the sun stands in the evening, there was an animal, worthy of a hunter. The chief had had a special weapon made for anyone who would try to slay this beast; it was a heavy staff which stood outside the house in case anyone had a fancy to test it.

Wander-hawk, who was never afraid, immediately decided to set out. But this time his wife came tearfully and begged him to remain at home. She was afraid she would lose him. Wander-hawk would not let himself be deterred by a frightened woman, and went across the country, up over the mountains. Far inland between these mountains he set eyes on a smoke; he took it to be steam rising in the frosty air from the surface of a river and went on. He walked and walked, and as he came nearer he saw that the smoke came from a big white animal; its whole body was covered with rime, rime from its own breath, so powerful were its lungs. Wander-hawk tested his staff, and as he thought it a little too long he cut a bit off. Then he went boldly towards the monster, who saw him and immediately came galloping. Snow flew from its nostrils. It snorted and shook the rime off so that its whole black body was bared. Wander-hawk braced himself and received it with the staff right in the forehead, exactly between the horns. It lowered its head and tried to butt, but Wander-hawk let himself be lifted on the powerful muscles at the nape of its neck and avoided the attack by leaping over the monster with a high spring.

The animal had stony scales all over its body; it was stiff and could not turn quickly, but Wander-hawk discovered that the scales parted a little every time it stretched its neck. The monster turned round, and again he sprang over it in the same way, letting the beast itself lift him; but this time, as soon as it bared the scales of its neck, he drove the staff into its neck and wounded it deeply. Thus he stabbed the animal many times, and when he discovered that the abdomen had no scales either, he stabbed it there too. Blood spurted out, the surrounding snow was dyed red, his very clothing became all soaked with blood. At last the animal bled to death and fell down. But this time the contest had been so hard that Wander-hawk was angry with his father-in-law.

It was late evening when he came home, and again there was song in the feast house. This time Father-in-law was absolutely certain that his son-in-law was killed, and the latter came in at the very moment when he was being reviled in song. But he leaped into the house with a powerful spring, drove the staff into the floor just in front of Father-in-law, and cried:

"Let your wife go up and fetch the meat of the animal you asked me to kill."

And there he sat, the young fellow, dripping with blood, blood all over his body, but without a single scratch.

The animal was never fetched, the meat never eaten; but Wander-hawk, who thought it the most dangerous beast he had yet slain, went up one day to see what its stomach contained. He cut it up, and it was packed with human bones.

It was a regular monster, a hidden beast of prey, an evil creature of the kind Wander-hawk wanted to root out.

.

THE DANGEROUS GAME OVER THE PRECIPICE

SUMMER came, and there was again big hunting for all kinds of game. Father-in-law was seldom in his own home, but mostly in the feast house or with other people. He was now afraid of his son-in-law and did not dare to live with him.

In the autumn all the men of the settlement went up to a high mountain, a steep mountain wall with a deep precipice below. Here they played the game of the precipice. A large tree trunk was dragged up to the top of the mountain and laid so that the root was turned away from the precipice, and the trunk stuck out over it. The men lay down over the roots to hold them, and one by one took turns in balancing out upon the trunk. Whoever lost his balance fell into the precipice and was killed. All the men had tried it, and now there was only Wander-hawk left. He balanced out, but when he was well over the precipice his old father-in-law gave a signal previously agreed upon: *"Keke!"* Immediately all the others sprang away from the root, and the trunk toppled over the precipice, taking Wander-hawk with it. Father-in-law laughed heartily and cried to the young men: "He who reaches my daughter first shall have her."

Now all the young men ran a race to the settlement, tumbling in through the passage to be the first to reach the young woman; but when they came into the house, Wander-hawk was already sitting on the bunk, chatting and laughing, just as if nothing had happened to him. Hovering over the precipice he had changed himself into a wander-hawk and had been home for a long time. And all the young men sneaked out foolishly without saying a word.

WANDER-HAWK IS BURNED TO DEATH IN THE FEAST HALL

ONE day, when they were in the feast hall, all the men suddenly rushed out, and before Wander-hawk realized what was happening he discovered that the entrance was barred. The feast hall was set afire and burned down quickly. When the whole house stood there like a smoking ruin, Father-in-law said as usual: "He who reaches my daughter first shall have her."

Again a race. All the young men darted off to be the first. But when they came into the house Wander-hawk sat on the bunk and jeered and laughed with his wife.

When the fire surrounded the feast hall he had changed himself into one of the maggots that was also his amulet, a little creeping thing nobody noticed, and thus he had crawled out through a chink and run home to his wife

The only result of the fire was that all the men of the place, at great trouble and inconvenience, had to gather timber and build themselves a new feast hall.

WANDER-HAWK FIGHTS SINGLE-HANDED AGAINST ALL THE MEN OF THE SETTLEMENT

One day when Wander-hawk was sitting alone in the feast hall a man came in and said:

"Make yourself ready for fighting. All the others in the place are making arrows to fight against you."

"Let them do what they like," answered Wander-hawk, but nevertheless began to make arrows. He was scarcely ready when they cried through the window that he was to come out. Outside, all the men of the place were gathered in a long line, and they shouted mockingly to Wander-hawk that he was to take sides with his party. His party was himself—he was quite alone against all the others.

And now they took to shooting at him, but with no avail. His fly amulet worked; he was never anywhere they thought he would be when they sent off their arrows. At last all his opponents had shot off their arrows, and now it was Wander-hawk's turn. Now he could get at them at last. And so he shot them one by one, never missing. Even those who tried to escape were hit.

At last there was only Father-in-law, who tried to hide himself, embarrassed like a little shamed child.

"This time you shan't be spared," shouted Wander-hawk, "but you aren't worthy to die by bow and arrow." And so he seized a stick and struck him down. First he broke one arm, then the other; then one leg, then the other, so that the wicked father-in-law could neither hold his hand before him nor walk. Then he stripped all the clothes off him and flung him naked into the feast hall. There he burst doors and windows so that the cold came right in, and let him lie broken and impotent on the floor, where he froze to death.

WANDER-HAWK RETURNS TO THE WOODS

So WANDER-HAWK stamped out all the evil men who had assailed him, and when ten days were past, in which he might do no work after the manslaughter he had committed, he went hunting again.

He dragged together caribou after caribou, and piled them up near the settlement, and all by himself he kept the women and fatherless children abundantly supplied with food and clothing. Both sea and land animals did he slay, and he towed many white whales into the settlement.

A year passed. Then he began to fill the plains round the houses with caches of meat, and when he thought that he had collected more meat than could ever be consumed, he decided to return home. He left his wife behind, although she had borne him two sons; but in farewell he gave them beautiful beads as lip ornaments. And so at last he traveled homeward towards Silivik. He still met many people, but none that were dangerous, and he was only cruel and hard towards those who were evil.

At last one day he reached his old home, his father's and mother's dwelling. But vainly did he seek for them, vainly did he call them. They were nowhere to be found. They were both dead. And Wander-hawk sat down in silence on the ruins of their tumble-down house.

Now he was home again, after having fulfilled the task his old father and mother had given him. He had traveled round the whole world, for he had gone from Silivik to Ko-buk River, and from there to Noatak River and the country of the Indians. He had sailed down the great Yukon River, and from Norton Sound he had gone across country to his old dwelling. Everywhere he went he had avenged his brothers. He avenged them by uprooting all that was evil and ugly, all that threatened men with malice and igno-rance. And now, when he had finished the long journey and had done what was required of him, he mourned deeply that the old folk were dead, the old folk for whose sake he had accomplished all his exploits, Father and Mother, whom he had sought to gladden. Grief overwhelmed him. He felt him-self lonely among men and empty in his mind, just as his home had now become empty. He climbed the slopes by the strand and looked once more over the country where he had played as a child. The sun was just going down behind the

He changed himself into a swift wander-hawk and soared high
over the mountains

mountains, and the last red rays fell over the plains, where he had hunted caribou, and over the sea, where he used to encounter white whales and young bearded seals. He swallowed his tears and straightened himself to his full height. Here he had nothing more to do. And so, taking refuge as usual in the powerful amulets which his father had given him, he changed himself into a little, swift wander-hawk.

In hasty flight he soared high up towards the blue sky, over the mountains, and disappeared in the self-same woods from which his father had once emerged.

And here ends his history.

Told by Old Nasuk from Kotzebue.

Printed in the USA
CPSIA information can be obtained
at www.ICGtesting.com
LVHW041738280124
769859LV00015B/176